PENGUIN BOOKS

HOW TO BE GOD

George Mikes was born in 1912 in Siklós, Hungary. He studied law and received his doctorate at Budapest University. He became a journalist and was sent to London as a correspondent to cover the Munich crisis. He came for a fortnight but stayed on and made England his home. During the Second World War he broadcast for the BBC Hungarian Service where he remained until 1951. He continued working as a freelance critic, broadcaster and writer until his death in 1987.

In 1946 he published *How to be an Alien* which went into thirty editions and branded the author as a humorist writer, although he had not intended the book to be funny. His other books include *Über Alles, Little Cabbages, Shakespeare and Myself, Italy for Beginners, How to Unite Nations, How to be Inimitable, How to Scrape Skies, How to Tango, The Land of the Rising Yen, How to Run a Stately Home* (with the Duke of Bedford), *Switzerland for Beginners, How to be Decadent, Tsi-Tsa, English Humour for Beginners, How to be Poor, How to be a Guru* and *How to be a Brit*. He wrote the historical study, *The Hungarian Revolution*. He is also the author of *A Study of Infamy*, an analysis of the Hungarian secret political police system, *Arthur Koestler: The Story of a Friendship* and *The Riches of the Poor: A Journey round the World Health Organisation*. On his seventieth birthday, in 1982, he published his autobiography, *How to be Seventy*. Many of his books are published in Penguin.

Marie-Hélène Jeeves studied architecture at Cambridge University and illustration at Cambridge College of Technology and St Martin's London. Since then she has worked as a cartoonist and illustrator for a variety of magazines and newspapers including *Harpers and Queen, Architect's Journal, Homes and Gardens,* the *Observer* and the *Sunday Express Magazine,* and for several publishers. Her book illustrations include *Supertips I* and *II* (Moyra Bremner), *The Nouveaux Pauvres* (Nicolas Monson and Debra Scott) and *Awful Moments* (Philip Norman). Marie-Hélène Jeeves has exibited in London with other cartoonists at the National Gallery, the Camden Arts Centre and the Cartoon Gallery where she has also held a one-woman show. She has exhibited in a touring show of the Ikon Gallery, Birmingham. Her interests include gardening and playing the cello. She is married and lives in Hackney.

GEORGE MIKES

How to be God

Illustrated by
MARIE-HELENE JEEVES

PENGUIN BOOKS

Penguin Books Ltd, 27 Wrights Lane, London w8 5tz (Publishing and Editorial)
and Harmondsworth, Middlesex, England (Distribution and Warehouse)
Viking Penguin Inc., 40 West 23rd Street, New York, New York 10010, USA
Penguin Books Australia Ltd, Ringwood, Victoria, Australia
Penguin Books Canada Ltd, 2801 John Street, Markham, Ontario, Canada l3r 1b4
Penguin Books (NZ) Ltd, 182–190 Wairau Road, Auckland 10, New Zealand

First published by André Deutsch 1986
Published in Penguin Books 1988

Printed and bound in Great Britain by
Cox & Wyman Ltd, Reading

Contents

————◆————

What Uncle Sigmund Missed

God is indispensable. That's why humanity, at the dawn of its existence, created Him: not God as He later became, but God in innumerable, diverse and often rather primitive forms.

Whatever His form, God had to be the *Universal Explanation* (of thunder, lightning and so on for primitive man, and of more complex phenomena for man who is slightly less primitive – i.e. us). He also had to be the *Great Protector*, with a personal interest in our fates; the *Stern Disciplinarian* who punished primitive man for eating more than his fair share of the buffalo, and Victorian schoolboys for playing cricket on Sundays; the *Source of All Wisdom* (however insane his ordinances might appear); the *Epitome of Beauty and Goodness* (however dubious the evidence for the goodness); and the *Supreme Guide* who, in every circumstance of life, whether pleasant or horrible, showed the Way and laid down the Law.

There is a conclusion to be drawn from all this, and how it escaped the attention of Sigmund Freud is a puzzle. Freud was one of the immortal giants of mankind (a wild exaggeration, of course, since mankind itself is not immortal); one of the Great Five who changed the fate, the outlook and the consciousness of humanity. (These were Jesus, Newton, Darwin, Einstein and Uncle Sigmund – three Jews and two Englishmen, which ought to mean that Jews and Englishmen are the finest specimens of humanity and that *English Jews* are the crown of creation. But, fine people though English Jews are, they are not the crown of creation, and this is not only because the Americans, the Germans, the French, the Bulgarians, the Japanese, the Fijians and everyone else are all convinced that *they* are the crown of creation, but also because there was no creation, consequently it cannot have a crown.)

Sigmund Freud said many profound, revealing and often frightening things about God, and also about Mothers; yet he failed to see the connection between the two.

The first God in every baby's life is its mother. She is the *Universal Explanation*, the *Great Protector*, the *Stern Disciplinarian*, the *Source of All Wisdom* and the *Supreme Guide*. God was not born of a virgin, but all virgins, male and female, are born of a God.

When the growing human child realises, to his sorrow and bewilderment, that his mother is not God, he starts searching for a substitute God: a plain-clothes God, or a God in disguise.

All my life I have been a great feminist: an admirer of women's bodies and brains, acknowledging their equality with, and often superiority to, men. It is true that in the last few years the antics and downright stupidity of some extreme feminists have disillusioned me a good deal, but in one respect I have to agree with the extremists. If the idea of God grew out of the relationship between babies and their mothers – if God is an extension of the Mother-ideal – then God must be a Woman. From now on I shall call Him *Her*.

It is often said nowadays that God is in a decline. This is nonsense. God cannot be in a decline because – as I have said – She is indispensable. God is omnipresent as ever She was – but She has become less easy to spot. In the Middle Ages, for example, there was One God sitting up in Heaven, instantly recognisable by everyone; but nowadays She takes many forms and we have any number of Supergods, ordinary Gods and mini-Gods.

We all go through a certain amount of trans-substantia-

8

tion during our lives. A mean man becomes Meanness itself; a giving man becomes in himself a Gift; a poor frightened soul becomes Fear. The Hungarian poet Gyula Illyes published an admirable poem in 1956, during the uprising, in which he described how he who lives under tyranny – inhaling and exuding fear, suspicion, despair, anxiety, and loss of individuality all day and every day, and even in his dreams – eventually becomes Tyranny itself. Similarly, human beings, in their constant search for God, try to become God. Most of them succeed.

In this book I shall show how this is, or ought to be, done: in other words, How to be God. It is something which, in fact, most human beings know already, although instinctively rather than consciously. God Almighty, up there, is not – however – so relaxed and comfortable in Her job. So at the end of the book I shall respectfully offer Her my humble advice.

The God Complex

There are millions of people all over the world whose knowledge of psychology consists of two words: *inferiority complex*. Most of these people haven't got the remotest idea what an inferiority complex really is, they do not know *to whom* one ought to be inferior, neither do they know how the idea of the inferiority complex was born nor who its father was.

Its father – at least its putative father, who claimed paternity – was Alfred Adler, the great Viennese psychiatrist and educationalist. He often said: 'After all, I am the father of the inferiority complex' – a child many people would not be particularly proud of.

(Adler was a great man but not quite a giant of Freud's stature. Without Freud Adler's Individual Psychology would not exist. And the same goes for Jungian psychology too. Adler and Jung – like quite a few others – rose to world fame not only because of their achievements but also because they quarrelled with Freud – the easiest thing in the world to do. Adler was a warm-hearted and likeable person and could write better than both the other two put together.)

Adler's most famous thesis is this: the basis of all neurosis is an inferiority complex; or, to be more precise, an uncompensated feeling of inferiority. 'Every neurotic,' he wrote, 'has an inferiority complex. No neurotic is distinguished from the others by the fact that he has an inferiority complex and that the others have none. He is distinguished from the others by the kind of situation in which he feels unable to continue on the useful side of life.' Adler adds that to tell a man that he suffers from an inferiority complex is no more useful, no more therapeutic than to tell a person who has a headache: 'I tell you what's wrong with you. You have a headache.'

So the neurotic feels inferior. But inferior to whom? Lewis Way in his book on Alfred Adler explains that there is no objective measure of this inferiority, it all depends on a person's own evaluation of his circumstances. The neurotic may feel that he is not equal to the demands of Life. 'He has looked at his organ inferiorities or his position as the younger or elder or only child.' He may feel inferior in sexual matters; he may feel that his mother pampered him or spoilt him, that his mother did not allow him enough freedom or did not care for him sufficiently, or that he comes from a poor family, or a boringly middling one, or that his father was too rich and too eminent. Whatever the case, he is driven to the conclusion that he can never be strong, capable and adequate enough.

Adler is absolutely right but he does not go far enough. Or perhaps he does, but fails to say so in so many words. He does not enunciate the conclusion that follows from his premises. As *every human being* is either a younger, elder or an only child; as *everybody's* mother allowed him either too much or not enough freedom, as *everybody's* father was either rich or middling or poor, *all humanity* suffers from an inferiority complex. Putting it in less high-falutin' language: we are all a bit nuts. This is not proclaimed by the Viennese school of psychology; yet it is absolutely true.

Like any other truth it is proved by exceptions. As people in Budapest liked to remark in my day: 'We perfect people are few and far between.' But we exist. I and you, Gentle Reader, are well-balanced and totally sane, always on the creative side of life, free of envy and jealousy. That makes two of us. But everybody else – without a single further exception – is a bit nutty. In the words of a memorable *New Yorker* cartoon: they do not have an inferiority complex. They are inferior.

Adler's second mistake is just as grave if not graver.

Few people (in fact only you, Gentle Reader, and I) are prepared to admit their shortcomings. They compensate for their inferiority by being arrogant, loud, tyrannical, domineering, competitive and aggressive. Everybody's feeling of inferiority drives him to a desperate desire to achieve superiority. The superiority complex (says Adler) is just the reverse side of the coin. And this superiority is not real, it is a mirage, a dream; it is self-deception. The feeling of inferiority is the real thing, the striving for superiority is a desperate and vain antidote.

And here again Adler fails to go far enough. Most people's inferiority complex is not merely a matter of feeling slightly inadequate, or not quite up to it; it is – at least on occasions – a feeling of being utterly and hopelessly useless. They do not suffer from a simple inferiority complex but from a full-blown nothing-complex. And a nothing-complex needs an all-powerful antidote: a God-complex.

. Every human being strives to be God – as he envisages God. Everybody's God is different from everybody else's God. God is not unique; there are as many Gods as there are human beings.

In addition to the divine characteristics described in the previous chapter, God is also immortal, omnipotent, infallible, superior to all other beings, dominant over all others, wise, good and noble. Briefly, She is exactly as we all want to see ourselves. Indeed, as we all *must* see ourselves, to overcome that nasty nothing-complex lurking at the bottom of our souls.

We follow many different roads. The ideal God, as we have seen, is different for each of us. But, essentially, we all chase the same dream. Atheists do not believe in the divinity of God Almighty. But everyone – whether atheist or believer – clings to the notion of his own divinity.

Stephen Pile wrote a charming and witty piece on David Frost in the *Sunday Times*. He said that Frostie's wife – at that time his fiancée – Lady Carina, the Duke of Norfolk's daughter, informed her favourite nun that she had found the man she wanted to marry. Mother Wilson frowned and asked if that man, David Frost, was religious. Lady Carina replied: 'Oh yes. Very. He thinks he is God Almighty.'

This was the most human touch in Frostie's profile. If he is God, he is human.

"*. . . exactly as we all want to see ourselves.*"

More Divine than Thou

However hard we all cling to the notion of our own divinity, that tormenting old nothing-complex continues to lurk at the back of our minds. (Now that I have discovered it I think it ought to have a more dignified name: let it be known as the *nihility complex* – a complex of feeling nil.) Fiercely though we try to compensate for it, the nihility complex remains an agonising and harrowing spectre which must be exorcised.

If someone has to feel like nothing in comparison with a brother, a sister, a playmate, a competitor, that is unbearable. But if the comparison is made with something of the utmost magnificence, an omnipresent, omniscient being of limitless power . . . well, that's quite another proposition. And there lies another reason why we had to create God. The more glorious and august our creation, the easier it is to bow before it. Make your God big enough and you can bow before Her without losing face – you can humble, humiliate and abase yourself, you can call yourself Nothing. Think how often congregations of worshippers announce in their prayers and psalms that they are unworthy specks of dust, crawling worms, heaps of . . . well, heaps of nihility.

What they really mean is that only God (who they have created) is more wonderful than they are – which is not humility, but arrogance. Martin Luther, for example, was undeniably a repulsively arrogant man, yet he was deeply humble and self-effacing vis-à-vis God. What Luther meant was this: He (in Luther's day they still called Her

Him) – He must be something superlatively marvellous if even I bow my head to Him and acknowledge His superiority. *His* superiority yes – but no one else's.

A human being so uncommon that he or she was not tormented by a nihility complex, would not insist on being superior. He would acknowledge his fallibility, he would be aware of his faults and weaknesses; but not – I repeat: not – of his insignificance. No one is insignificant. And no human being – or God – is more important than any other human being. A real human being does not crawl in the dust – however strong his nihility impulse may be. He does not grovel in front of any creature, existing or invented, human or divine.

He will try to improve himself. But he will feel no need to improve God in order to be able to accept the fact that someone may be more divine than he.

Our Infinite Goodness

———◆———

God is not only a creation but also a projection of Man. He is ridiculously anthropomorphic. God is not what Man is but what he would like to be. God is what Man, the eternal Walter Mitty, sees himself to be.

First of all, God is good, so all men want to be good. Or more precisely: as all men want to be good they have created a God of infinite goodness. If you are aspiring to divinity – and who isn't? – you must be good. You may be a thief, a murderer or a robber baron but that does not prevent you from regarding yourself as a good man. I have never met a cunning thief, a cruel murderer or a ruthless robber baron – and I have met many such people – who was not convinced of the whiteness of his own heart, his own true goodness.

No thief regards himself as a thief, a criminal. He has to live. If society is mean enough to deny him a proper livelihood he is entitled to support himself in a slightly unorthodox manner. Being a burglar, as he sees it, is just a job like being a lawyer, an M.P. or a stock-exchange speculator – except that it's a little more honest. It is a basic injustice that some people have more money than he has, so he must rectify this injustice. The owners of vast houses, famous jewels and renaissance masterpieces may or may not be more deserving than he is, but this has nothing to do with the case. Some are better, others are worse.

Isn't he a good father? A good son to his aged mother? Doesn't he like his dog and his budgie? Doesn't he love flowers? What makes a good man, after all? Obeying a few stupid, unjust, outdated laws, or to being a good and kind family man?

Every man is good in his own eyes. Terrorists are good men, devoted to a just cause and ready to make tremendous sacrifices for it. If completely innocent passers-by, many children among them, are killed by their bombs, that does not really matter. They, too, are making sacrifices for a just cause.

Some terrorists can be a bit selfish, though, acting for personal gain rather than their cause. Religious leaders of various persuasions have been known to promise boys of fourteen or fifteen (and also people who are older, but no less immature) that they only have to blow themselves up to find themselves in heaven enjoying eternal bliss. And these ayatollahs and so on must be right: there has never been one single complaint. Not one boy, girl, or child of more advanced age has ever come back to remonstrate: 'I say, you promised me the most glorious seat in heaven, near the feet of Allah and surrounded by the heavenly host, and nothing of the sort has happened. I am rotting in a ditch, dead as a dodo, and I shall be forgotten in a fortnight.'

People readily accept that *other* people may be evil. To take a famous example. Stalin was sincerely convinced that kulaks were bad people. He believed that *every* kulak was bad, and (quite logically) that everyone bad was a kulak. It was he who decided – in perfectly good faith, of course – who was a kulak. Whether or not it actually gave him pleasure to kill sixteen million people – we cannot be sure about that – he knew that it *had to be done* for the world's good. His energetic pursuit of this sacred task was to leave Soviet agriculture in an even greater mess than it was in when all those kulaks were alive and happy, so it is possible to argue that Stalin sometimes failed to foresee the future with precision – even that he was not incapable of making a slight mistake from time to time. But about his *intentions* there can be no question: they were pure and noble.

Hitler was an equally well-intentioned man (*equally* is the key word). A Jew once spoke to him disrespectfully when he was a nobody in Vienna, and as a result of this it was then and there revealed to him that Jews were evil and must be exterminated for the benefit of mankind. He was not so much *against* Jews as *for* the rest of humanity which – because he was such a good and great man – he had to save. Six million Jews had to die, but he meant it well. And if we remember that he did not even know what was going on, we must see that in a complicated sort of way he was an even better man than he seemed to be at first. It was over-zealous underlings who did it all, and they in their turn were all virtuous men who were acting on orders from their superiors, who were even more virtuous because they had never given any such orders and hadn't the faintest idea of what their underlings were doing. With so much sincere virtue about, it is clear that six million Jews managed to die just in order to besmirch Hitler's good name. And anyway, Hitler loved his dog.

If even mass murder can be committed for the benefit of humanity, you can see how easy it is for the smaller and more ordinary kinds of wrong-doing that most of us favour to be harmless – or, indeed, virtuous. The truth is that search as hard as you may, you will not find a speck of wickedness – or even of nastiness – among any of the divine creatures who inhabit our earth.

Two Good Deeds

It may sound like a boast but I am not a good man myself.
I can count the number of my good deeds on the fingers of
one hand. Indeed, I do not need to use a hand. I can count
them on my ears. The total number of my good deeds is
two.

I have described one of these good deeds in an earlier
book (*How to be Seventy*) but as it is relevant to my subject I
am going to tell about it once again.

In 1955 I went to Wells, in Austria, and wrote two
articles for the *Observer* about refugee camps there. The
little series was called 'Forgotten People'. Refugee camps
are rarely cheerful places but the Wells camps were
particularly dismal and heart-breaking, full of human
wrecks and rejects. Most of the inhabitants were Yugo-
slavs but there were quite a few Romanians, Hungarians
and Bulgarians among them. They were nearly all sick and
elderly. The young and healthy ones, particularly those
with useful skills, were picked out and sent to the United
States, Canada, Australia and other desirable countries.
Sweden was the only country to take a number of sick
and blind people; for the other countries 'helping refugees' meant helping themselves to a few well-trained and
much-needed young and healthy specialists. Many of the
people I met at Wells had been there for years and few had
any hope of getting out. A few were still optimists, busily
collecting documents and visiting consulates, only to be
told that more and more documents were needed, or to be
turned away with a few kind words. Or unkind words.

One day after the Hungarian Revolution of 1956 (which I had covered for BBC television) I travelled to the Hungarian frontier and stopped at the bridge at Andau. It was not much of a bridge any more. It was broken down and people were squelching through the slush to reach Austrian soil. There had been an invasion of people, a veritable flood, but by the time I got there the flood had dwindled to a trickle – but there were still people arriving. I stood there, watching them wading through the mud, exhausted, almost collapsing, yet happy. Suddenly someone standing on the bank beside me greeted me by name. It was an old man and he asked me if I remembered him. No, sorry, I did not. He was Mr Horváth. The name did not mean a thing to me – it is a common name in Hungary. He reminded me that we had met in Wells. Then I remembered, all right. 'Forgotten People', I thought: I had forgotten them just as everybody else did. How was his wife? I asked him. She was there – and he pointed to a frail little woman, standing a few steps away. He dragged a huge pile of documents out of his pocket.

'I've got almost everything now,' he told me proudly. 'Just one more to come. Perhaps two. They won't be difficult to obtain. Then we are off to the USA, to Cleveland, at last.'

Two more documents, I thought. How often had I heard that. Then two more. No one ever had enough documents, if he was old and sick.

'A very different proposition for those,' he said, looking at the newcomers without bitterness. 'They just come over and are asked: "Where do you wish to go?" They say: "The United States." Or "New Zealand." And a week later they are there.'

I asked him: 'May I give you some advice, Mr Horváth?'

'What is it?'

'Go back to Hungary.'

He stared at me, obviously thinking I had gone mad.

'Go back?' he asked with horror.

'Yes. Not far back. Just cross the frontier here, it is quite easy and not dangerous. Go behind that large bush over there. And tear up all your papers. Burning would be better, but tearing up will do.'

He still thought I had taken leave of my senses.

'I have spent years and a lot of money collecting these papers.'

'Never mind. Just tear them up. All of them. Don't keep any souvenirs. Not even the most precious ones. When you've got rid of them, come across the bridge – or whatever is left of it . . . through the mud. With your wife. As new refugees. And when they ask you where you wish to go, say Cleveland, Ohio.'

He looked at his wife who had come nearer and was listening. She nodded. A fortnight later I received a postcard from them (via the *Observer*) from Cleveland, Ohio, USA. And eleven years later I received another postcard from Mrs Horváth, telling me that her husband had just died. She obviously thought that my good deed – which involved cheating the authorities – had contributed to his last years of happiness in America.

* * *

My other good deed was very different. In 1949 I went to Israel to collect material for my book, *Milk and Honey*. I spent a lot of time with members of the British Embassy in Tel Aviv. On the whole they were not a happy lot. Some of them loved Arabs and disliked the Jews. Others were full of goodwill towards the new state. But whatever their attitude they were not popular. The War of Liberation was just over and the British were accused of having done everything in their power to secure an Arab victory. Ernest Bevin was Number One in Israeli demonology. But this general unpopularity was not the main reason for the unhappiness of the British Embassy. The main reason was that they had no chance of playing cricket.

'We have an eleven here,' I was told, 'but what's the use of it? There are no opponents. Who plays cricket in Israel?'

During my peregrinations I went to a kibbutz in Upper Galilee where the majority of members had come from England – there were quite a few Londoners among them, but most of them had come from Manchester. They were breaking stones (in those days kibbutzniks still had a hard life). Most of them had served in the British Army in the Middle East. After the war they returned home, were demobilised and then went back to the new state of Israel. They led a hard life but they had no regrets. Yet they were not altogether happy. They offered me a cup of tea. I replied that I wanted no tea but a cold, iced drink, *gazoz*, the national drink of Israel in those days. 'We have no *gazoz* here,' they told me. 'Have a nice cup of tea.' I saw copies of the *Manchester Guardian* but no Hebrew language newspapers. 'We are trying to learn Hebrew,' they explained, 'but we are not much good at languages.'

One of them added: 'Our children will be taught Hebrew. And Hebrew only.'

The others nodded. Someone added: 'And, of course, English.'

The chief reason for buying the *Manchester Guardian* (as it then was) was to be informed about the fortunes of Manchester United. And also of Chelsea.

'A great difficulty is,' one of them called Gershon told me, 'that we also love cricket, but we cannot play the game here. We have an eleven but no one to play against.'

Should I dare to speak out?

'We are not very popular here with the other Israelis,' Gershon continued, 'because we are regarded as English. They blame us for Bevin.'

'That's unfair,' I suggested.

'Not altogether. We voted him in.'

I thought I ought to tell them about the British Embassy and *their* cricket eleven. But I did not. Back in

Tel Aviv I told the story to my friends at the Embassy. They gave no sign of being delighted, but all the same they must have approached the kibbutz in some round-about way, because first I heard that neither side was eager to meet the other – indeed, both were quite reluctant – and later the news reached me that love of cricket had proved stronger than this mutual distrust, and they had enjoyed quite a few good games. I am still pleased with my Good Deed Number Two (which was Number One in chronological order).

Thinking back on it, I am not sure that it was simply their love of cricket that brought these people together. Perhaps the unpopularity they shared had something to do with it, not to mention their common madness. It is hardly surprising that people who choose to drink hot tea instead of iced drinks in the blazing heat of the Middle East should end by playing cricket against each other in the midday sun.

Power

———◆———

Man needs power. All men need some power and they all have some. Power is a primary need and that is why Man made God all-powerful.

Reflecting on power we can see how weak and forlorn the seemingly powerful often are; and how powerful many of the so-called grey nonentities may be. We also see that power has its laudable aspects, but the kind of power with which humanity has invested its God is ugly and repulsive.

Lord Acton's famous dictum about absolute power corrupting absolutely is inaccurate, simply because there is no such thing as absolute power – not if the word *power* means the ability to achieve your own ends. It is a word which makes us think, first of all, of the great tyrants of history. Stalin's power could not prevent him from being a frightened man, always trembling for his life, unable to rid himself of a paranoid anxiety. He did not even dare to taste a spoonful of soup at home in the Kremlin until a guinea-pig had tasted it for him. Hitler's 'absolute power' achieved the defeat and disintegration of Germany, the establishment of Israel as a free and independent state, and the conversion of the Germans (for a few years at least) into the most despised and hated of races or – to use his own terminology – the Jews of the world.

Or look at that tinpot Caesar, Arthur Scargill, President of the National Union of Mineworkers, the instigator of the famous and disastrous miners' strike of 1984. His power is not quite on the level of Stalin's or Hitler's but his

26

megalomania seems to rival theirs. And he achieved – comparatively speaking – the same success for his union as Hitler achieved for Nazi Germany. This is the picture at the time of writing: he drove his members (not all of them) into an illegal and criminally violent strike; he caused horrible misery and suffering to his loyal and decent miners; he split the union and caused almost irreparable internecine feuds and bitterness; he squandered the union's funds and the union's financial control is in the hands of the receivers; he lost the strike without achieving anything. True, he himself considers the whole affair as a glorious and historic victory, and his loyal followers made him, after all that, President for life, so he salvaged something from the disaster; but not, surely, what he was aiming for.

So the powerful seem, in the end, to be powerless. Of those we have considered, Stalin fared the best, but even he was thrown out of the history books of the Soviet Union, and of his own crypt into the bargain.

It is another interesting phenomenon that many of the great tyrants, from Stalin to Hitler, from Idi Amin to Bokassa, were clinically and certifiably mad: poor deranged creatures whose childhoods must have been sadly deprived, since we all know that unloving mothers are responsible for everything. I know nothing about the mother of Djinghis Khan, but she cannot have been a cosy woman, she must have given little Djinghis the impression that she was rejecting him. When social workers called, no doubt she fobbed them off with feeble excuses which – naturally – they believed without hesitation. You can't blame a child, after that, if he goes out and devastates Asia and Europe.

I understand *him*, but why do millions of seemingly sane people follow these mad Djinghises and Hitlers and Idi Amins through misery and disaster? This apparent mystery is easily explained. First, the mad tyrant, as a rule, has the magic gift of the gab and promises his people in a highly convincing way that he will lead them to victory and glory. Not a word does he ever say of the ruin and tragedy which will in fact be the end result. Secondly, a nation (or any other large group) may consist of sane individuals, but as soon as they become a crowd, a mob, a rabble, and feel the influence of a brilliant orator who is seemingly invincible, they go just as mad as any tyrant.

But let us leave tyrants. No one but the most wretched outcast has no power at all – even the next-to-most wretched outcast has the power to share or not to share the crust he finds in the gutter with the most wretched. Ordinarily, if someone is kicked around in the outside world he will go home and kick around his wife and children. If he cannot do this because, for example, it is his wife who kicks him around in the first place, then he will kick his dog. And the dog will chase cats, the cats will kill birds, and the birds will pounce on worms.

There is a charming little verse by the nineteenth-century Hungarian poet, Sándor Petöfi, about a shepherd who receives the alarming news that his sweetheart is dying while he is riding his donkey (his feet reaching to the ground). He races back to the village as fast as his donkey can carry him, but he arrives too late, the girl is dead.

> What can he do?
> He's mad and sick:
> He beats the donkey
> With his stick.

Not an effective rebellion against heavenly injustice, but a pretty universal way of achieving immediate, if momentary, relief.

Although it is the great tyrants who come to mind first when one is thinking about power, I suspect that servile people are even more dangerous. The cumulative harm done by the slavishly obedient may well end by exceeding the evil done by tyrants, although their activities are less conspicuous and are often dismissed as unimportant. Obedient and servile people flatter and kowtow to their superiors; they bow deferentially and fulfil orders; and in this way they establish hierarchies. Once the idea of obeying the person above you is fixed in your brain, then it becomes obvious that you must be obeyed by the person beneath you. The sadistic old-fashioned sergeant-major with new recruits at his mercy is typical of this phenomenon: his blind obedience to the officers gave him, he was sure, the moral and legal right to bully and torment his victims.

Humanity has often been seen as falling into two groups: those who lead and those who follow. The leaders are supposed to be power-hungry, or at least born to lead, while the others are born to obey. But it is not so simple as that. In the first place almost everyone is a link in a chain and is rewarded for obeying his superiors by being allowed to kick around those below him – indeed, his obedience is often merely the price he has to pay for ruling over his own slaves. And in the second place, those who obey a leader often do so in the hope of achieving power through the group formed by his followers. A tremendous sense of power is often enjoyed by those who submerge themselves in groups and give up their individuality in order to carry on in ritual ways – chanting slogans, wearing uniforms (whether conventional or outré), and indulging in threatening gestures such as the goose-step.

But of course people who seek reassurance in groups are not the powerful beings they fancy themselves to be. They are whistling in the dark because they are scared and unsure of themselves. The truly strong person is the one who dares to walk alone; the one who – although he is frightened – faces the mob, or turns his back on it, with determination. The truly powerful person is the nervous philosopher, the frightened thinker, the one who – like Galileo – makes a dangerous discovery or who – on a very different level – refuses to join a trade union. To utter

unpopular views when surrounded by howling conformists is a lonely and alarming activity – nearly all the great spiritual heroes of humanity knew what it was to be terrified – but it demands genuine power, not play-acting.

Power has become a dirty word, but it should not be so. First, as we have seen, all of us need a bit of it and pretty well all of us have some. A basic necessity cannot be entirely evil. If we substitute the word 'authority' the dirtiness more or less disappears (only 'more or less', because 'authority' is too closely associated with the idea of authoritarianism). There are many people with inborn, dignified authority of a kind which makes it likely that they will be chosen as leaders of their parish or their nation. (It is a fact that when a jury has to choose a foreman there is rarely any doubt about who it will be: eleven out of twelve people will almost always recognise at once that the twelfth is the person for the job.) These people are not, as a rule, power-hungry, cruel or bullying. They are picked to take the lead in the same way that an exceptionally good actor is picked for a star part. (Their power and success may end by spoiling them, but that is another matter.)

It is interesting to observe that God is not this acceptable type of leader. She is all-powerful and whimsical, and Her ways are so daft that they have to be dignified with the word 'mysterious'. She is unforgiving. She is sly (think how often she supports *both sides* in a war, at one and the same time). And she is very unjust, often allowing the wicked to prosper while the innocent go through Hell. We must remember that none of this is a reflexion on Her. It is a reflexion on us. We could have created a perfectly decent and lovable God if we had wanted to.

The Greatest Power of All

The second famous dictum about power, after Acton's, comes from Stanley Baldwin. He said that power without responsibility was the privilege of the harlot.

'Harlot' is a delightfully old-fashioned word and this is a delightfully old-fashioned idea. Baldwin was making a political point about the press barons. Less colourfully expressed he simply meant that power should be wielded responsibly. His colourful remark, however, is untrue even on the political level. Power without responsibility is not the privilege of the harlot but the privilege of the tyrant. The adage is also untrue on a general level. *Lack of responsibility* gives one tremendous power – something approaching Acton's absolute power.

I have recently heard about a picturesque London family – one of many of this type – which takes pride in being a bunch of crooks, thieves, liars and shoplifters.

Not long ago their twelve-year-old boy (just to give an example) was carrying an enormous bag full of groceries down the street. The local policeman – who knew the whole family only too well – stopped him and asked what was in the bag. 'Groceries for Granma,' the boy replied. As his Granma did live nearby, the policeman let him go – and then heard, a little later, that a lady's shopping (a whole week's shopping for a family of six) had been stolen in the supermarket. So he visited Granma and made enquiries: had she received some groceries from the boy? Yes, indeed, her grandson had carried home a heavy bag of them for her, so that her son could take it up to Leicester to give to her daughter, who lived there. He had just driven off. She did have a daughter who lived in Leicester, so what could the police do? They could not even ask for a search-warrant.

The technique is simple: there is always a grain of truth in all their lies, which creates confusion and makes them difficult to pin down. If one lie happens to be exposed they smile innocently and cover it up with three others.

They are petty criminals, of course, not murderers or terrorists. But their complete lack of responsibility, the fact that they suffer from, or enjoy, complete moral insanity, makes their lives easy. It is not that they are 'getting away with it'. Oh no. From their own viewpoint they are simply 'making monkeys' of authority. They know the rules of social security payments and entitlements better than many a lawyer. They get huge sums out of the Department of Health and Social Security – some of it even legally – and have a good laugh at them. They enjoy life immensely, all the time. They are clever and the authorities are stupid – that is what they feel, and this feeling makes them happier still. More than happy: invulnerable.

The boy attends school when it suits him or when he has nothing better to do. Teachers are helpless. If he is expelled from one school he shrugs his shoulders and so do his parents. One more worry for the authorities.

Many a dangerous and much more vicious criminal has a pang of conscience every now and then. This lot does not know the feeling of guilt at all. And even if a big-time gangster is not really worried by a feeling of guilt, he is often afraid of being caught – he can't relax. Not this family. If they are occasionally caught – well, it's bad luck, part of the game, part of the fun. Going to prison has no stigma attached to it. He who goes to war may be wounded. They are released soon enough and then pick up the threads where they left off.

They are truly happy people. They are financially well

off, they eat good food, have their tellies, videos, family cars and if they need a second car they steal one or 'borrow' one and abandon it when they have finished with it.

No one has any power over them: no law, no policeman, no priest, no local authority, no government. They are more powerful than any Prime Minister. They cannot fall. They need not fear their backbenchers or a vote of no confidence. As no one has any confidence in them to start with, they cannot lose anybody's confidence.

They – and a few thousand others like them – are as near to enjoying God's total power as any man can be.

Money

When I was collecting material for my little book on the United States, *How to Scrape Skies*, I chatted with a second-hand clothes merchant somewhere in Lower Manhattan. He declared in a loud voice and with shining eyes that God had made America perfect. (Meaning, of course, the United States – the rest of America doesn't count.) As I failed to respond with equal enthusiasm, he remonstrated with me: 'Well, what about it? Don't you agree? What's wrong with you?'

I was anxious to avoid an international incident, so I replied diplomatically: 'Well, God has made America a fine country. A very fine country, indeed. But not perfect.'

He thought this over and found it a sound basis for compromise: 'OK. God made America the finest country on earth. And He could've made it perfect if only He'd had the money.'

I have now recalled this well-considered statement and, on reflection, it strikes me as strange that God has no money. Not a penny; not a cent.

Why is this? Is it because God was created by primitive desert-dwellers, hewers of wood and drawers of water, thousands of years ago, long before Mrs Thatcher's market economy, at a time when barter was the means of exchange? Or a little later, when power meant rank, land and the possession of cattle but money was unimportant? God certainly has the most exalted rank and is the master over the life and death of all sheep and cows, but She has not got a farthing to Her glorious name. Had She been

created in the twentieth century, She would be fabulously rich, a multimillionairess, the platinum taps of Her bathroom embellished with huge diamonds, rubies and emeralds. She would have countless Rolls Royces with telephones, televisions and ice-boxes for Her champagne.

Or is She without money because She knew that the New Testament would contain the phrase: 'Blessed be ye poor: for yours is the Kingdom of God.' It would not create a good impression if people were encouraged to remain as poor as possible while God Herself was immensely rich. If that were so She would not be one of the blessed; nor could Her own kingdom belong to Her.

Or – another possible explanation for God's shaky financial status: She has no idea of the value of money because, like Francis Joseph, erstwhile Emperor of

Austria and King of Hungary, She never goes out shopping and has everything She needs without ever visiting a grocer's or a branch of Marks and Spencer.

For many years Francis Joseph – a small deity himself in his own realm between 1848 and 1916 – had a close relationship with Katalin Schratt, an actress of Vienna's Burgtheater. They grew old together. The Emperor had a secret passage built from the Burg – his palace – to Mrs Schratt's residence, and used it every day. One day Mrs Schratt showed the Emperor a beautiful ring which she had just bought. The Emperor admired it dutifully.

'What d'you think it cost?'

He looked at the ring once again, very carefully and said: 'A hundred crowns.'

'But Franzl!' shrieked the lady, 'a hundred crowns! Do you know what it really cost? *Ten thousand.*'

The Emperor re-examined the ring even more carefully and declared: 'Not expensive. Not expensive at all.'

First he thought it was a hundred, then he found ten thousand not expensive at all. Obviously, deities, of whatever calibre, are not well informed about current prices.

Or perhaps all these suppositions and theories are misconceived. Maybe God in Her ultimate wisdom, simply despises money too much to touch it. She, being omniscient, read my book, *How to be Poor*, a few millennia before it was written and was convinced by its arguments.

In that book I did not advocate Biblical poverty, only the reasonable, comfortable, lukewarm, middle-class poverty in which most of us exist. But I did deplore the vulgarity of money and the vulgarity and misery of the rich. I also deplored the futility of fortunes because, as a rule, rich people do not own their money and their possessions but their money and their possessions own them.

This fact creates a painful contradiction. For most people money does not mean just money: it means power,

love, the outward sign of success. But God knows better. She is wiser than her creator, Man.

Her Churches – almost all of them – while propagating poverty for others and promising the poor the Kingdom of Heaven, used to grow immensely rich. This was slightly embarrassing. The fact was swept under the carpet. During the Middle Ages – particularly at the time of the Avignon schism – the upper echelons of the Christian clergy declared it to be heretical to demand that the Church remain poor. St Francis was one of the few who got away with it; not easily and not entirely, but his order, though detested and condemned by many, survived. Nowadays we do not hear so much about the beauty and virtues of poverty and about whom the Heavens belong to. We have the rich Churches on the one hand and on the other hand the poor congregations and a penniless God.

The arrangement cannot be changed. Too late for that. Too much has been said in the past. The Churches try to twist and bend the facts as much as they can, but in the same way that Communist lies are (so Communists assure us) the *real* truth, so the riches of the bishops are *real* poverty. *They* are rich; God is poor. A comfortable arrangement. They have the best God ecclesiastical money can buy.

Minigods

The real difference between the God in the sky and the Gods on earth is that human Gods are much more modest. More real too, but mainly more modest. The various Gods in the sky – Christian, Moslem, Jewish, Shintoist, Hindu etc – rule the entire world (which, somewhat surprisingly, means merely this wretched, tiny provincial planet of ours). Human Gods are satisfied with ruling their immediate surroundings, however small and insignificant an area that may be. In many cases one single, miserable subject satisfies them: they can kick him (her) about, torment him (her) and make clear who the master (mistress) is. The sun in the sky shines with blinding brilliance, exuding an almost unimaginable amount of energy, but even so may be covered up by a few clouds; but in a completely dark room the light of a single match dominates and enlightens the place and when that match goes out, darkness reigns again.

Human Gods are on to a good thing: it is your immediate surroundings that count. A hatmaker I knew was once involved in some sexual misdemeanour and fined £200. His case was reported in the *News of the World*, readership at that time twenty millions. He shrugged his shoulders. But when a similar news item appeared in the *Hatmakers' Times* (or whatever that trade journal is called) readership eight hundred, he became suicidal. His judgement of values and relative importance was perfect. It did not matter if a few thousand miners in Durham and fishermen in the Hebrides, who had never heard of him, read about the case. They saw a name and forgot it in a few seconds. But it made all the difference in the world if eight hundred hatmakers, who all knew him personally, learnt that he was in the habit of exposing himself in the Ipswich–Liverpool Street train. *That* was the real exposure.

Similarly, few people play a part on the world stage. It is their offices, wives, children, colleagues, club-mates, fellow trade unionists who matter. A person wishes to be the cleverest, the brightest light, the highest authority in *his surroundings*, not in the whole, wide world. So he doesn't waste time on dreaming of being an Emperor, but he becomes – for example – a teacher. I do not say that all teachers are led to their profession by this desire, but many are. Nor do I say that a modern teacher has all that much authority. But even today small children still believe that Teacher is an admirable person who knows everything better. It is easier to play the part of God among five-year-olds – and even among fourteen-year-olds – than in an illustrious gathering of people, with IQs of 180 and over.

Judges are almost pushed into divinity. They cannot help deciding people's fate and fortune and are surrounded by people who keep kowtowing to them. *Kowtow*, or *kotow*, means, according to the Oxford Dictionary: Chinese custom of touching ground with forehead as sign of worship or absolute submission. This seems to me casual and almost offhand behaviour compared with the treatment allotted by barristers to our judges. The Chinese simply expressed absolute submission to a superior human being; the barristers' constant braying of 'As Your Lordship pleases' reflects total submission to a divine Lordship. The judges wear medieval fancy-dress and a wig which may be clownish but which nevertheless distinguishes them from ordinary human clay in its jeans or suits bought at John Colliers. Barristers, as far as dress is concerned, represent a half-way house between clowns

41

and civilians. You cannot blame judges if they start believing in their own divinity. Indeed, I admire quite a few of them who have remained almost human, and I know at least one who is still decidedly modest.

Medical doctors are another divine lot. They hold the key to physical existence. They may cure or kill. Killing is a lot easier, but they do often cure, too. It is fashionable to decry medical knowledge and deride physicians but this is unjust. They do know a lot and learn more and more every day. They are a conscientious lot and my complaint against them is not that they kill too many people but that they do not kill enough. To be a little more precise: they do their damnedest to keep alive sick people whose life is nothing but misery, pain and suffering and whose only wish is to die. The doctors' determination is due partly to the Hippocratic oath and partly to a more modern Hypocritic oath. Hippocrates of Cos lived some 2,500 years ago and his teachings are about as relevant to modern medicine as the teachings of the Bible or the Koran are to modern life. Besides, most of the books attributed to him were, almost certainly, not written by him. The Hippocratic oath is confused, unclear and thoroughly un-Hippocratic (in the sense that it has little to do with the old boy). The second reason for the doctors' attitude is the misplaced pressure of society which declares that human life is sacred. Human life is not sacred. Human life is very precious, it should be protected by all possible means and the medical profession on the whole is doing a magnificent job. But if a life – through tragic misfortune – becomes worthless, then, quite obviously, it cannot remain precious at the same time. Particularly if the one and only desire of the sufferer is to die. A suffering person's well-considered and deep wish may be sacred; to keep a human wreck alive against his or her will is cruelty, practised in the name of a quack who died two and a half millennia ago.

A week before I came to write this part, my dear and

much loved little cat, Ginger, fell suddenly very ill. I took him to the vet who suspected peritonitis and told me that this was fatal. Nevertheless, he added, Ginger would be X-rayed. If his diagnosis was right, Ginger should be 'put to sleep' because his life would be very short in any case, and sheer suffering. He told me to ring him at six in the afternoon. I did not ring at six but went there at four. Ginger was dead. He did not have peritonitis but died of cancer: his chest cavity was filled with blood and other fluids, so his lungs became infected and he could not breathe. This was a bitter blow to me. I loved Ginger and he loved me. All the same, I was glad to know that he did not suffer much, that his life had been happy during the last seven years he spent with me – and he was conscious of his happiness. I was even gladder that, after all, I did not have to pronounce his death sentence . . . which, however, I *would* have pronounced, with aching heart. The question, which lingers on in me, is this: why do we 'put to sleep' our pets while we deny a dignified exit to those of our fellow-humans who want it? Why do we treat cats better than people? Just because, in most cases, cats deserve it more?

Reverting to the divinity of doctors: it is fed by another source, too. The doctor is the Knower of Secrets. And to make it worse: the Knower of *Your* Secrets. The kidney may be yours but it is he (he thinks) who knows what is wrong with it. He may tell you. On the other hand, he may decide not to, because you are a layman, too stupid to understand and in any case, it is none of your business. Only your kidney. Poor doctor – let us be fair – is a very busy man, usually with a formidable load on his shoulders, and he cannot spend his time giving long lectures to all the patients in a huge ward. Yet there seems to be something wrong with this division of labour. Whose business is what? The patient's business is to get better or to die. Learning and practising medical science is the doctor's business.

The other day I heard a story which could have been invented by a modern Aesop, but in fact it is true. It comes from Israel. A reasonably well-to-do lady from Tel Aviv visited a famous specialist, a University Professor in Jerusalem. She told him that she had been seen by two Tel Aviv doctors who recommended an operation. She would like to hear the Professor's views. 'So you want a third opinion?', the Professor said. 'Fair enough.' He examined her and in the end declared: 'Yes, I fully agree with my Tel Aviv colleagues. You must have an operation.'

The lady replied: 'Thank you very much, Professor. But I won't have an operation.'

'Why?'

'I'll tell you why. Because I am afraid of it.'

The Professor looked at her for a while and then asked: 'May I ask you: how did you get here from Tel Aviv?'

'By bus.'

'And who drove that bus?'

'An extremely good-looking young man, with long hair.'

'I see. And you entrust your life to an extremely good-looking young man with long hair whom you have never met before, but not to an eminent surgeon?'

'Oh, the difference is enormous. That young man *was travelling in the same bus*.'

* * *

Clergymen are the representatives and agents, the errand-boys, of God on earth. Their closeness to the Almighty makes them half-divine, they feel.

However, one does not need to select special professions – teachers, doctors, clergymen – to meet the God complex in full bloom. Many people of every rank and status wish to shine and dominate others. One dustman (usually the driver) rules the team; one chap in a two-men office; one man – or woman – in a two-person marriage; one beggar on a two-beggars-site. The ruling and dominating will give him (her) more pleasure than work, marriage or begging. One miserable subject is as good to rule over as a whole country. And that one single miserable subject, as a rule, is quite happy about being ruled and dominated although usually unaware of his pleasure.

The masochist needs the sadist, he is lost without him. It is not always realised that the sadist needs the masochist equally badly. In many marriages the tormented wife will occasionally threaten her sadistic husband that she will leave him. 'Good riddance,' he will reply. 'The sooner you clear out the better.' He says that in the certain knowledge that she will never go; he even means it. But sometimes she does go. And then the poor sadist is lost. The content, the purpose, the essence of his life has disappeared. He will run after his wife, beg her to return, promise that he will change and mend his ways. The wife will return and for one week (maximum) all will be well. Then the old pattern will reassert itself. The sadist must be God; the masochist must be martyr. The sadist cannot live without his victim; but the martyr equally needs the Inquisitor who burns her on the stake.

And that is the key to the whole phenomenon. Man (meaning human beings) cannot conceive his relationship to others on a basis of equality. The mistaken explanation for this is the superior outcry: 'Of course not, because people are not equal.' No, they are not equal. But you can *treat* other people as if they were your equals, even if they are your inferiors. Or your superiors – as the case may be. In all human relationships there must be bosses and underlings, masters and slaves, rich and poor, officers and other ranks, rulers and subjects, beggars and donors, Gods and mortals. God owes Her very existence to this human need. Man wants to identify himself with the Boss, the Master, the rich, and with God; only a few wish to identify themselves with the slave, the poor, the beggar and the unemployed.

God is not the master of humanity yet humanity is afraid of becoming the master of God. It is high time for Her to join the ranks of millions of others and become the Great and Immortal Unemployed.

On the Benefit of Mutual Contempt

A few days ago, in a village in Devonshire, I went to buy a newspaper. In the window and on the stands outside I saw picture postcards, a few paperbacks, and packets of sweets but, when I asked for a newspaper, the woman in charge told me most snootily: 'We're not newsagents.'

Her demeanour was reproachful and resentful. She was telling me off. What did I take her for? Hers was an insignificant little shop, selling everything else usually sold by newsagents, but her claim to fame, her social standing, her rank in society was apparently based on the glorious fact that she was *not* selling newspapers. That lifted her into a different world, into a rarefied atmosphere.

It would not have occurred to me to look down upon that lady because she was selling newspapers. But, however hard I tried, I could not admire her for *not* selling them. That, in my eyes, was a lesser achievement than it was in hers. Most people are not really proud of their achievements. They are proud because they are proud. They were born proud and that's that. They are proud of what they are – whatever they may be.

Once I heard a small, suburban estate agent tell a holiday story to a friend of his. The gist of it was that somewhere on the Costa de Something, he and his wife received rather off-hand treatment during the first week of their holiday but real VIP treatment during the second week.

'That happened, of course,' the suburban estate agent

explained, 'because at first the hotel people did not know who we were.'

His friend gave him a wry look and asked: 'And who *are* you?'

A pertinent question, which only a few people care to ask themselves.

People are proud of their nationality, their colour, their name – things they have not chosen, so they have little reason to be proud of them. Country people are proud of not living in filthy towns like London; Londoners are proud of not being country bumpkins. Intellectuals look down upon businessmen but that is nothing compared with the contempt businessmen mete out to intellectuals. Some patrons of restaurants look down upon waiters and all waiters look down upon their clients. Mr Smith is proud of his name (and a good, simple, honest name it is) but everyone with a complicated, treble-barrelled name will look down upon Mr Smith. The contempt, probably, will be mutual. Mr Smithe, Psmith or Smyth will, of course, deny that his name is really Smith with a touch of affectation added to it. People living at the posh end of a street will look down upon others living at the poor end, and vice versa. The rich look down on the poor, the poor on the rich; English on immigrants and immigrants on the English; butchers look down upon mere 'meat-merchants', specialists upon GPs; barristers practising in the Chancery division look down upon criminal lawyers, bus drivers upon conductors, physicists upon engineers, pure mathematicians upon applied mathematicians, video-repairers upon television-repairers and so on *ad infinitum*. (And people who can use expressions like *ad infinitum* look down upon others who cannot.)

All of them may be right, of course. The people they despise may all be pretty contemptible. Or they may not be. But there is a complicating factor in this equation. It is just possible that the television-repairer lives at the right end of the street while the superior video-repairer lives at the much less posh end. Then the TV-repairer will look down upon the video-repairer because of where he lives, while the video-repairer will go on despising the TV-repairer for not being a video-repairer. The 'meat-merchant' may have a much larger and more expensive car than the highly qualified butcher and the GP may bear a more distinguished name than the consultant. *All* the classes, at least in Britain, hold one another in mutual contempt – in other words: *everybody looks down upon everybody else*. The sole problem is finding the right angle for your despising. Mutual contempt is a firm basis of true democracy. Humble reverence of the 'great' leads to a hierarchical society and a slave mentality. Contempt is the solid rock on which democracy is built – but it must be universal and mutual.

The reader may object that I have veered from my original subject. I am not talking about the God-complex but about common or garden snobbery. Yes, I am talking of snobbery, but snobbery is the father of the God-complex.

Our adoration of God is partly sheer snobbery. We call our secular monarchs 'Your Majesty', being fully aware of the fact they are not intrinsically more majestic than anyone else. It is his title, our adulation, his palaces, his guards in splendid uniforms, our calling him 'Your Majesty' which makes a king pretty majestic – more majestic than most of us. It is not the saint who radiates the halo; it is the halo that makes the saint.

It follows from all this that God has the best address: *Heaven* is even better than Buckingham Palace, SW1. She is the richest – even though She has not got a penny. She is a specialist in everything – a butcher, not a mere meat-merchant. The purest mathematician and the greatest of all engineers. And She has the most distinguished name, too. She does not need to spell it Gode or Godd. She is the ultimate incarnation of Total Snobbery.

The Power of the Weak

What about those who appear to have no power at all? What about the infirm, who must rely on others?

Many of them are tremendously powerful. The power of the weak can be very nearly absolute, and it is also extremely destructive.

We have considered some of history's monstrous tyrants, but there have also been a few who were benevolent and who did good. Peter the Great was no angel, but Russia was more advanced and more European at the end of his rule than it was at the beginning. Frederick II, also called the Great, gave his Prussians good reason to tack that adjective onto his name. Views differ about Cromwell, but many historians rank him among the greatest Englishmen. Lower on the scale, it is possible for over-strict fathers, didactic bosses, loud-mouthed army officers or ruthless business managers to have good sides to them and to produce beneficial effects. Sadistic husbands are often caring and generous – indeed, it is a characteristic of the sadist that as long as he can lay down the rules and his wife (or other victim) dances to his tune, he will be jealously protective.

Perhaps the only tyrant who never shows that redeeming 'other side' is the weak tyrant. His, or her, effect on the victims subjugated by helplessness is destructive and nothing else.

Most of us play the weakness game from time to time, and bring kind or showing-off people to our aid by appearing at a loss. Advertise how helpless you are at carpentry, and it is quite possible that your neighbour will drop in with timely aid for the fiddly bits. Drop a few dishes while washing up ('God, aren't I clumsy!') and you may well – what joy! – be forbidden ever to do the washing up again. But the power of the weak can be far greater than that. If someone shouts at you you can always shout back. If someone is vicious and nasty you can be more vicious and even nastier – even if it calls for a great effort on your part. But if someone moans and cries out for your help, you are enslaved. You may walk out on a tyrannical parent but you cannot walk out on a sick one, however unreasonable and demanding he or she may be. Or you feel you cannot. You can, of course, but very few people have the nerve to do so when their aged mother tells them she will die without their constant attention – particularly as aged mothers often mean it and would willingly die just to spite their offspring and give him or her a feeling of guilt for the rest of his or her life.

Many people who sacrifice their lives for an ailing relation believe – persuade themselves – that they do it willingly; that they undertake this duty voluntarily, because they love Dad, or Mum, or Marjorie, or Uncle Hugo so much. They do love them. They also hate them. They are terrified that they may die. They are even more terrified that they may stay alive. And, most of all, they are terrified of their own secret and suppressed desire that they *should* die and hurry up about it. No man has a claim on another person's life. A life sacrificed for another is a wasted life. Sick, feeble, old, invalid people ought to be treated with care, kindness and sympathy. But many of them demand – and their victims offer – full lives as sacrifices on their own altar, and that is monstrous. 'Whose life is it anyway?' asks that excellent and memorable tragicomedy, meaning that a man has the right to do what he likes with his own life even if he wishes to terminate it. Yes, he has a right to his own death. But he has a right also to his life.

Your life is yours and no one – not even your nearest and dearest – has the right to claim it for himself. 'But what if he dies? . . . What if he becomes unbearably miserable?' It is only his selfishness that makes him miserable. I am no paragon of noble self-sacrifice but if I knew that I was spoiling somebody else's one and only life, *that* would make me unbearably miserable. I would not accept it under any circumstances – and I know that many people feel the same way. One should accept help, of course, and sympathy, and a certain amount of someone else's time. But a life is too much to claim – yet so many people claim it. And so many foolish people offer it, grinding their teeth, thinking themselves noble and unselfish, and hating their beloved.

But – you ask again – what if the weak tyrant dies of misery at being looked after by strangers in a hospital, or in some sort of home? Many people are happier in old people's homes than at home. Others are happier being alone. But alone means alone and not with you.

Yes, yes, all this is obvious, but you ask again: what if he dies unless you look after him day and night?

We are all going to die one day, why shouldn't he? But he is unlikely to die. He wants to live out his God-complex, he wants to rule over at least one person and he will do that as long as God gives him sufficient weakness.

* * *

It is not only parents and elderly relatives who wield the overwhelming power of weakness. Children, too, often discover it. Cunning babies learn in no time to abuse their terrific power.

The child of well-to-do parents who goes shop-lifting and steals a bar of chocolate he could easily afford to buy is not a vicious little monster but a desperate little soul crying out for help and love. In the overwhelming majority of cases he wants to punish a parent for lack of love, for neglect, for parental tyranny, for some concrete injustice, and this is the only way he can do it. Perfectly well-meaning parents cry to heaven: 'What have I done to deserve such a child?' It is a good question. Instead of paranoid outcries he should examine his relationship to his child. Cruelty, neglect, lack of love, tyrannical rules or often the other extreme: over-protection, pampering, too many protective rules, too much attention – never leaving the child alone – are, in a sense, worse crimes than stealing a bar of chocolate.

I specially remember one such case. The parents went on blaming their fourteen-year-old 'incorrigible' son, who went on stealing. The parents were desperate but they failed to notice two things. The boy always stole utterly useless things (useless to him): tins of vegetables, potato peelers, apple-corers, flea-powder or, in bookshops, Sanskrit grammars or books on the Use of the Dative in Eleventh-Century English. And he always took the utmost care to be discovered. If he was not discovered – he

54

confessed. He did not confess because he felt contrite but because he felt vindictive. He did not steal in order to *have* the stolen goods; he stole to embarrass and embitter his parents. His parents were strong, wilful, upright people, why did they have such a wicked boy? But the boy was not wicked, of course. We all need power and he used the only power he had against the strong, wilful and upright parents. The terrifying, near-divine Power of the Weak.

Opting Out

God is never alone. Not that She would be lonely. She has, of course, enough of what we call inner resources.

And Christian God is part of a Trinity, into the bargain, so She could not be alone even if She tried to – which fact may put Her omnipotence in doubt. But She does not try, and neither do any of her rival deities in Heaven. She needs her admirers around. It is the human concept once again. What is the point in being admirable if you are not admired? Man created God as vain as himself, so God is surrounded by creatures who keep telling Her how wonderful She is. Those admirers must be terrible bores and they are turning God into a real show-biz personality.

If God is never alone, why does Man, who created Her, often 'opt out'? The answer is: he does not opt out as often as he seems to do.

There are, admittedly, a few genuine hermits. Sometimes they live in a cave in the country (there aren't many caves in cities), but often they live in city flats among millions of other people, yet in complete loneliness. Many other people are simply left alone because no one wishes to see them. These are the involuntary hermits, living in *loneliness*: the true hermits are never lonely: they live in *solitude*.

The *double hermit* or *dual hermit* is a modern phenomenon. The double hermit is a couple, perfectly satisfied with each other's company and not too fond of the rest of humanity. Possibly, the rest of humanity is not very fond of them, either. All the same, as a rule, the double hermits are self-sufficient and intelligent people. They have the best of both worlds: they are alone yet they enjoy the company they want.

The man who is 'opting out' is a bit of a cheat. He is trying to cheat, first of all, himself. He turns his back on society, claims to despise it, turns away from conventional social life, scorns all honours (which are not offered to him in any case) and regards social life, politics, religion, capitalism, socialism or whatever, as a sham. So he joins a tiny, off-beat, often lunatic sect. But, of course, he is not opting out; he is opting in. .

Few people play a part on the world stage or even on the national stage. Those who do cannot possibly opt out. Someone who hopes to become President of the United States, or a Member of Parliament in the United Kingdom (or even in a Communist country where he may be assured of 98.7 per cent of the votes once he stands) must remain part of society.

But those people who have tried to play a part in their community, or at least in a close circle, and have failed, often decide to opt out and, consequently, opt in. What I mean is very simple. The person becomes, say, a punk rocker. He turns his back on our undeserving society, which fails to appreciate his sterling qualities, and seeks the warmth and camaraderie of a small, closed group. He shaves half of his hair off and dyes what remains of it purple – not because he believes that half-shaven half-purple hair is beautiful, but because that is the price for being allowed to opt in. He must conform to strict rules, just as a barrister must wear striped trousers and a wig in court. This is the way to superiority. There is a firm belief that any group which despises or rejects the rules and traditions of more or less decent but often dull society, is superior to the common clay.

As purple hair is still relatively uncommon, Punk Rockers are noticed. And as not too many white men shave off *all* their hair, put on an Asian night-shirt and chant psalms in Piccadilly, the Hare Krishna people are noticed too. The list could be continued. They may look

57

foolish – they may indeed be fools – but they are noticed. They were fools before they started on their antics, but in those days they remained unnoticed. People desperately want recognition. Most of them prefer being recognised idiots to being unnoticed nobodies.

This simple desire is the driving force of Punk Rockers, Moonies, Scientologists, football hooligans and rich people who must have golden taps in their bathrooms. It also motivates those who slavishly follow half-crazy prophets, completely crazy ideas and cynical dictators of fashion. Even mass suicide, committed by several hundred people, is a desperate attempt at opting in – it is considered much better to die in a blaze of worldwide publicity than to live a dull and insignificant life. The warmth of small groups which consider themselves superior can be very comforting. The ghetto meant seclusion and humiliation but it also meant warmth, togetherness, the company of like-minded people belonging to the same race or family, the absence of hostile strangers and prying eyes. The walls of the ghetto were always defended from within with as much determination as they were barred from the outside.

Apartheid is a gloomier and even more repulsive phenomenon than the ghettos of the Middle Ages, but even apartheid seems to have its peculiar fascination. During the 1985 Labour Party Conference (and agitation had started earlier and went on afterwards) there was an acrimonious debate: many black people wanted to establish special black sections in the Party. They wished to lump together blacks and Indians – who have very little in common and usually detest one another – and call themselves *coloured*: a phrase I find insulting. In a previous motion the same people vociferously condemned apartheid; in this one they were determined to establish a private, cosy apartheid of their own.

To belong to your own ghetto is one of the basic human needs. Down with apartheid! Long live apartheid!

Celebrity

———◆———

Not so long ago a man could become a *famous* writer, musician, architect, politician, sportsman, financier, actor, ventriloquist or whatever by being a *good* writer, musician, ventriloquist etc. . . . and this is still possible today, to some extent, but the real thing is to become a CELEBRITY. A writer may be famous because he writes good, or at least successful, books; a sportsman may be famous because he is the second best fast bowler in Lancashire. A celebrity is famous because he is famous: and the more famous he is, the more famous he becomes.

The species of Celebrity develops mostly, but not exclusively, on television. The chairman of a quiz programme is a typical Celebrity. He asks questions which have been put together by others; he could not answer any of the questions he asks for toffee. He becomes what we call a national figure just by reading out what is written on a card. However, he will never be quite so famous as a news-reader. Nothing ever happens to most news-readers except that they read the news, put together by others. They read quite fluently – only the brightest students in the fourth form of a comprehensive school read better. After retirement the news-reader writes his memoirs, describing his dull and uneventful life and his fleeting meetings with famous men who have sat next to him for two or three minutes during a news bulletin. His books will sell like hot cakes, better than, say, a new novel by William Golding – even if he cannot write half as well as he can read. People will besiege bookshops for his autographs and the book will be a great bestseller even if no one reads it.

There are innumerable other ways of becoming a Celebrity. For instance: undress at a football match and run around the pitch stark naked. It is quite easy, really. If you are a presentable young lady with a slim waist and big breasts and give a good chance to photographers to advertise your charms world-wide, you will become a Celebrity, will be invited to lecture on Egyptology or numismatics and – much more important – may even be invited to appear on television chat-shows.

If a sportsman achieves a world record or becomes a world champion – well, that's not bad. But if he throws tantrums, shows his bare behind to the spectators (who have come to watch other things) or attacks an innocent spectator he becomes a real Celebrity. Gorgeous Gussy, who wore frilly pants at Wimbledon in the fifties, is widely remembered – but few people would be able to tell you who the ladies' champion was in the Year of the Frilly Pants. You may be a pious and devoted clergyman and no one will pay the slightest notice to you. But declare – being a bishop – that you do not believe in the Immaculate Conception and the Virgin Birth, or in some other basic tenet of the creed which employs you as a bishop – and you become a great Celebrity (even if not a great bishop).

And talking of distinguished clergymen, many Iranian Celebrities come to mind. They are bigoted, cruel and bloodthirsty men, behaving much worse than our football hooligans (who are only minor Celebrities), thirsting for more blood, demanding more executions of adulterers or people who consume gin and tonic, and vying with one another in bigotry, fanaticism, stupidity and murderous tooth-grinding. Why do they go on like this? They are quite often not at all what they seem to be: many of them are good family men and kind neighbours, and some of them (not many) are even teetotallers. But they have simple minds, poor things, and it is only human that they, too, want to be Celebrities like Allah, the well-known God.

Mysticism

God is a mystical figure. This means that if we cannot explain what She does we say: 'His [most people still insist on Her being masculine] ways are unfathomable, beyond our comprehension.' If God is Goodness – quite a few people wonder about this – then why do little children die of cancer? Because God's ways are incomprehensible and killing children with horrible diseases is a mysterious manifestation of His infinite goodness. The Calvinists maintain that our fate is decided even before our birth. Some of us will be saved, others will burn in eternal hell-fire irrespective of what we do on earth. It does not matter how noble and virtuous you are in life, burn you will if the Almighty so decreed before you were born. Conversely, you may be a monster more horrible than Mengele, but if God ticked your name before your birth you will enjoy eternal bliss. Why does God act in such a seemingly unfair and unjust way? Her ways are neither unfair or unjust. All this is sheer and unadulterated Goodness, it's just that we fail to understand Her mysterious ways. I certainly fail to do so. I also feel deep sympathy for Her: just because Calvin was a cruel, humourless, bigoted and confused fanatic there was no need to besmirch Her name.

So there are no mysteries? Many of my readers will ask this question ironically. The answer to it is: no, there are no mysteries. Or more precisely: *all mysteries are herring mysteries*. I have told this story somewhere else but I must repeat it. It seems to be a simple anecdote but it is not; it is a basic principle of my life and it deserves to be adopted and accepted by millions. By all humanity.

The story comes from my old and dear friend, Emeric Pressburger who, in the twenties, was a young engineering student in Prague. He was not exactly starving at the time, but almost. A few years later he was a prosperous and successful film-writer in the employment of the legendary UFA company of Berlin and was sent to Prague on business. He arrived in his own elegant, fast red motor-car, determined to enjoy all the gastronomic delights of that then admirable city which he had missed before because of his poverty. His very first act was to buy some rollmops, a kind of pickled herring. He took the rollmops back to his hotel intending to eat them for breakfast next day. As the day happened to be rather hot and humid, and there were no fridges in hotel rooms in those days, he put his precious herring on the window-sill to keep it as cool as possible.

Next morning a chirpy maid woke him up, carrying his breakfast tray. She greeted him with a charming 'good morning', placed the tray on a little table, pulled up the blind, wished him an agreeable day and left.

Emeric got up and – with pleasant anticipation – dived for his herring. It was not there. He searched thoroughly but the herring had disappeared. What could have happened? Surely, that nice girl had not pinched his herring? Emeric quickly dismissed any such idea. He had a lot to do and could not spend too much time on this problem, fascinating though it was. In fact, he might have forgotten about the whole incident but for something unexpected which happened that evening. He returned to his room, found the bed turned back, the blind pulled down, the bed-side lamp switched on, everything beautifully prepared. He threw a glance at the window-sill . . . and there it was, his herring, exactly where he had put it. 'How odd,' he said to himself. But not worth puzzling over, and he would eat it next morning for breakfast.

But he did not. Next morning exactly the same thing happened. The same chirpy maid arrived and everything went exactly as it had gone before. Once again the herring disappeared. Once again it reappeared in the evening. And this went on for four days.

Eating the rollmops was out of the question by now, but Emeric was intrigued – indeed quite disturbed – by the mystery. On the fifth day, however, it was solved. At the bottom of the blind there was a flat bit, which fitted the window-sill, and the herring had been sitting on this. When the blind went up, up went the herring too; when the maid let the blind down, the herring regained its original position. Emeric is a little more inclined to believe in mysteries than I am, and was somewhat disappointed that one of the seemingly inexplicable puzzles of his life had been solved in such a prosaic way.

I had many arguments about mysteries with Arthur Koestler who, as the whole world knows, tended to believe, and was extremely interested in, the paranormal. I ridiculed his belief and he ridiculed my stubborn disbelief. I realise now that essentially we were in agreement. He did not fall for cheats, crooks, and humbugs – indeed he regarded them as major obstacles in the way of serious research. All he was saying was that there are a number of phenomena which we cannot explain with our present-day knowledge, so let us extend this knowledge and try to solve the riddles by purely scientific means. I fully accept this; but while Arthur was prepared to believe in – I think even hoped for – some paranormal, extra-terrestrial explanation, I always maintained – and still maintain – that all mysteries are herring mysteries, i.e. they will all turn out to have a perfectly simple, ordinary, sometimes ridiculous, explanation. And let's leave God out of it.

Crystal Ball

If people who love mysteries are not arguing that God's ways are unfathomable, so no man can understand them, they are maintaining that *they* do understand God's mysterious ways and that they, and only they, can interpret them for us.

Quite a lot of people fall for this. The Roman *sacerdos* predicted the success or otherwise of a planned enterprise from the entrails of oxen or sheep. If a sacrificial lamb happened to have peritonitis before its death a planned war was postponed. This rarely happened, because God's interests always coincided, according to these Roman priests, with the interests of the Roman War Office. (All the same, the Romans were more intelligent than we are. They found it astonishing that when one *sacerdos* met another they could refrain from bursting out laughing in one another's face.) Pythia, the Greek oracle of Delphi, was more cunning. Her predictions were so obscure that they could be fitted to any event, so whatever happened later her prophecies always proved to be correct. (They could, of course, be misinterpreted *before* the event, but that wasn't Pythia's fault.)

It is not any more ridiculous to predict a person's future from the entrails of a dead sheep than it is to predict it from the constellation of the stars at the time of his birth. The universe is immense – even our tiny solar system is almost incredibly huge. Venus may or may not be close to Uranus at a given moment but whatever the distance between them, their position at a given moment will not influence the business deals of a single individual on a tiny, provincial planet, thirty-seven years (or whatever) later. Nor will the distance between the two planets influence the fates of wolves and rattlesnakes, or have any bearing on the character of zebras or kangaroos on that same insignificant planet. (And if it is supposed to have influence on humans, why not on bears?)

Crystal-ball gazing is a trifle less foolish. What you see in a crystal ball has, at least, something to do with you: you see what *you* want to see or else what *you* are afraid of, and as your character may indeed affect your future, what you can see may possibly answer some of *your* questions.

A friend of mine, a beautiful and intelligent woman, was persuaded, much against her better judgement, to visit a famous fortune-teller. She arrived at a suburban house. In a simple room there were two chairs and a table with a crystal ball on it.

The fortune-teller, a fat, amiable and chatty Cockney woman, told her: 'You gaze into the crystal ball, dearie, while I pop into the kitchen to see if my potatoes are cooked.'

'Oh no,' replied my friend. '*You* gaze into the crystal ball and tell *me* whether your potatoes are cooked.'

The fortune-teller was taken aback.

'I can't do that, love.'

'If you can't tell me whether your potatoes will be ready next door in two minutes, how can you tell me how my future husband will behave towards me in New Zealand in eight years' time?'

And my friend swept out.

In the course of centuries sheep's entrails have given way to packs of cards, crystal balls or the movement of stars, but humanity still endeavours to tell its future from signs which cannot tell anything about it. Oracles have moved from Delphi to street corners, suburban kitchens or elegant drawing-rooms and people's fortunes are told for cash. The more the cash the happier the future.

The Bible has also been a source of predictions for about two thousand years. The Bible is the nearest relation to Pythia: you can read anything into it, and the opposite of anything. It usually says nothing in particular but large masses still believe in this nothing. Humanity has not become any more intelligent in the last two thousand years.

* * *

But the reverence for, fear of, and belief in, mysteries will persist for a long time yet. Computers will be involved to prove our progress. Computers will try to build a bridge between man's newly acquired brilliance and his eternal stupidity.

The explanation for this devotion to mystery is obvious. Mystery is the characteristic feature of all extra-terrestrial and supra-natural power (it has to be!), and the mystery-monger (*sacerdos*, soothsayer, astrologer, Bible- or Koran-commentator, Talmudist, witchdoctor etc) wants people to believe (and would like to believe himself) that he is in close contact with higher powers. His clients whole-heartedly and hopefully agree: he is the man who puts *them* into contact with God, the power of the stars, evil spirits, good fairies or whatever. The contact is a bit tenuous and remote but any contact with the Mighty Ones is better than no contact at all. This is all a natural part of the God-complex.

Mystery, as I have said, will go on flourishing and that poor, glorious and honest bit of herring will have to rot away on the window-sill for quite a while yet.

Coincidence

At one time I was collecting coincidence stories, and a friend of mine remarked: 'So, after all, you do believe in mysteries?' But I do not. Coincidences are sometimes amazing, but there is nothing mysterious about them: they are bound to happen according to the very logical and unmysterious laws of probability. Millions of tiny events occur to each of us every day. Some of these *must* coincide with other, unforeseen, events, whereupon they create a good story but no mystery.

A simple example which has happened to all of us. We have not thought of Matthew Brown for thirty-two years – not since we left school. Then, walking along Regent Street, suddenly and inexplicably we think of this half-forgotten figure of our childhood. And a minute later who do we meet face to face? Matthew Brown.

I dismiss the rationalising explanation, which is that we may have caught a glimpse of him before we became consciously aware of his presence. I accept that it was pure coincidence. But we think of so many people in the course of a day that once in a blue moon such curious coincidences are bound to happen.

No one would dream of telling you a story like this: 'I have not thought of Matthew Brown for thirty-two years – not since we left school. Then, walking along Regent Street, I suddenly and inexplicably remembered this half-forgotten figure of my childhood. And then – lo and behold! – whom did I meet a minute later? Arnold Simpson.'

That is a non-story, but it happens more frequently than the first version. My point is that the first version, although rare, is simply *bound* to happen from time to time.

On this strictly non-mysterious basis I did collect a few astonishing coincidence stories. Some were tragic, some were funny, and all were amazing. I should like to give here a few pieces from my collection.

My brother Tibor served in the American army during the War. His unit, the Tenth Mountain Division, was famous all over the United States. They were trained in the mountains of Colorado and used skis to get from one point to another. This was not exactly a skiing holiday, as often they had to cover fifty miles in one day or, even worse, one night. On top of it all, they had to carry heavy equipment on their backs. They were also trained as parachutists, being dropped from planes complete with their skis and heavy rucksacks. At the end of their long and arduous training they were sent to Italy where they saw no snow (or very little of it), never put on their skis and never used a parachute.

They fought their way up from the South to the North of Italy and by April 1945, a week or two before the end of the war in Italy, they reached the River Po. My brother was in charge of a small reconnaissance unit. They were ordered – about eight or ten of them – to cross the Po and find out one thing or another. They did cross the river and when the last man reached the northern bank a shot rang out. They all fell on the ground and looked round. It was Jonathan Smith from Muncie, Indiana, who first noticed a German sniper sitting on the branch of a tree. He took aim and, with his first shot, killed the man. The sniper fell on the ground with a heavy thump.

My brother waved his men on. They did their job, found out whatever they were supposed to find out and returned by the same way. The dead German sniper was still lying where he had fallen. My brother Tibor told Jonathan Smith from Muncie, Indiana: 'Jonathan, you shot him. Go and search him.'

They had to find out, of course, the identity and the unit of the man, their main interest being whether German reinforcements had arrived. Jonathan did his job and while he was at it, the others heard a loud cry, a cry of bewilderment and disbelief. What had happened was this: Jonathan Smith took out an unopened letter from the dead man's pocket. It was addressed to him – Jonathan Smith. The sender was Mrs Jonathan (Mary) Smith, Muncie, Indiana.

Now, this is pretty unlikely. The explanation came a day later and, as usual, it dispelled the mystery.

The Germans, a few hours before my brother's unit crossed the Po, had raided an American army Post Office: a rare event in those last days of the war, but it happened. Mary Smith was in the habit of writing two or three large pages to her husband every day and then posting the whole week's output in one large envelope. As a result of this the letter was quite bulky. The dead German took part in the raid and probably thought that this extremely thick letter contained dollars, so he put it in his pocket. Before he could open the letter he was shot dead by the addressee.

No miracle. Just a strange way of delivering letters.

* * *

My first wife is half English, half Swiss-French. During the war her mother, Renée, had the habit of ringing up her friends – other Swiss-French ladies – two or three times a week just to have a little chat. They discussed domestic affairs, difficulties with war-time shopping, what was available, what you could get on 'points', where you could get an egg or two, and so on.

One day Renée phoned Yvonne Shoreham-Webb. The Shoreham-Webbs were rich and had a domestic staff even in those days, but Mr Shoreham-Webb was senile and difficult, so the servants usually left after a short while.

Renée heard the telephone ringing. A totally strange voice replied which, in the circumstances, was not surprising. 'May I speak to Mrs Shoreham-Webb?' my mother-in-law asked.

'Certainly. One moment,' replied the courteous voice.

Yvonne came to the phone and the two ladies started chatting in their usual manner: availability of this and that, plans on how to spend their clothing coupons, the peculiar hand Renée had had at their latest bridge-party and other pleasant trivialities. At last, after twenty minutes, my mother-in-law began to take her leave. Yvonne asked in an irritated voice: 'Well, is that all?'

My mother-in-law was surprised.

'What else should there be?'

But Yvonne sounded quite furious: 'If that's all you wanted, what was so urgent about it? Why did you have to ring me here?'

'What do you mean "here"?' My mother-in-law was more and more astonished. 'Where did I ring you?'

'At the butcher's.'

Renée had misdialled one digit and happened to get Yvonne's butcher. She asked for Mrs Shoreham-Webb and as Yvonne was in the queue, the polite butcher called her to the phone. She was ankle-deep in sawdust wondering all the time about the extreme urgency of the call.

* * *

Before the war my uncle Csori lived in Brussels. He was a prosperous businessman and was engaged in negotiations with another businessman from Antwerp. They could not conclude their discussions but Csori said that this did not matter because in a short while he would be going over to Antwerp and they would be able to get on with their talk.

'I'll ring you up when I arrive.'

'Right,' said the other, 'but not before the middle of next month.'

'Very well. Actually it's in the middle of that month that I plan to come.'

'Good,' said the other man. He took a piece of paper from his pocket, wrote some figures on it, and handed it to Csori who put the piece of paper in his wallet.

In the middle of next month Csori went over to

Antwerp and took the paper from his wallet. It contained this number: 151–238. He dialled and asked for his friend.

'Speaking,' he said. Csori identified himself and the man asked in an astonished voice: 'How did you know my number?'

Csori found the question a little strange, but before he could say so the man asked him to come to his office at once. When Csori arrived, the man's first question was 'How on earth did you know my telephone number?'

Csori grew quite irritated: 'What on earth do you mean? We agreed in Brussels that I would come over to Antwerp. You gave me your telephone number, I dialled it and got you on the phone. What is so miraculous in that?'

'I'll tell you what is so miraculous. I knew that I would get my telephone today. Five minutes before you rang I myself did not know what my number would be. So I cannot possibly have given it to you. Show me that piece of paper.'

Csori handed it over. 'Here it is, quite clearly: 151–238.' The man nearly fainted.

'This is not 151–238. It's 15.12.38. It is the date: 15th December, 1938. It's the date before which I told you not to ring me.' Csori had dialled the date – and got his man.

* * *

In the fifties and sixties I wrote a few light-hearted travel books. The public for some mysterious – in this case perhaps truly mysterious – reason quite liked these books, and I loved them: they enabled me to travel all around the world, meet interesting people and make a living in an extremely pleasant way.

One planned journey, however, collapsed for reasons I no longer recall. So I had to think of visiting another country. I was urged to go to the Soviet Union. This was during the Khrushchev era, after the famous K and B (Khrushchev and Bulganin) visit to London. I was not very enthusiastic about the idea. I disliked the very thought of going to the Soviet Union, besides, I knew that I would not be allowed to move about freely, to contact people and see what I wanted to see. Nevertheless, I phoned up the Russian Press Attaché and enquired about the possibility of a visa. He asked me indignantly: 'But you don't want to write a book on the Soviet Union *in your style*?'

'I have got no other,' I replied. 'I would prefer to write in Leo Tolstoy's style but I cannot do it.'

There was a brief but definitely frozen silence at the other end of the line. Then the Press Attaché told me curtly: 'Come along at 4.30 in the afternoon a week today.'

I went although very reluctantly. I did not like going there and I did not want to be seen by anyone. But I did go. The Press Attaché told me curtly that it was no good applying for a visa, I would not get it.

'Why?' I enquired.

He was quite annoyed. He was not used to being queried. A decision was a decision and that was the end of the matter.

'No reason. There will be no visa,' he said, and stood to indicate that the audience was at an end.

I left the building, irritated and slightly confused. No, I was not keen on going to the Soviet Union but I resented being refused a visa. *I* wanted to reject *them*. I was walking along Notting Hill Gate and saw the *Evening Standard* being delivered to a newsvendor. I saw on the front page, in enormous letters:

MIKES AT MOSCOW EMBASSY

I was flabbergasted. It was terrifying how well informed they were. But a moment later doubts started creeping in. My visit to the Moscow Embassy was quite an important matter for me, but it was hardly front-page news for a semi-national newspaper. I bought a *Standard*. The story was about hidden microphones and other bugging devices found at the British Embassy in Moscow.

Sex

————◆————

The sex life of God is a delicate subject. As humanity has a most peculiar attitude to sex, it has messed up God's sex-life, too.

In this chapter I must speak of God as a male, because God is the father and not the mother of Jesus.

The Greeks and Romans were the last people who had a normal attitude towards sex. It is true that that admirable and witty poet, Ovid, was exiled by Augustus to Tomi (today's Constanza, in Romania), a dreary Black Sea outpost in those days, perhaps even drearier than today; and it is generally assumed that the reason for his banishment was his three books, *Ars Amatoria*, in which he taught people how to make love. (Two books for men, one for women. Why? Is it because men make love more often than women? Or is it because men need more instruction?) However, this assumption is wrong. Rome was not prudish and it would be difficult to find anything in Ovid's books likely to annoy Augustus. It is possible that the poet seduced one of the Emperor's lovers; it is also possible that the Emperor was impotent and wildly jealous of the poet's virility . . . and in neither case would this have anything to do with *Ars Amatoria*. Many biographers have said that his exile (which was never revoked) cannot be explained. Others maintain that Ovid knew something about the Julian conspiracy against Augustus and – for reasons of loyalty to friends – remained silent.

(I must interrupt myself for a moment. I have always been annoyed by the English habit of mutilating Greek

75

and Roman names. The name of the poet just mentioned was *Ovidius* and not Ovid. And Vergil or Virgil was *Vergilius*, and Homer was *Homeros*. *Cicero*, for some reason, has not been dubbed Cicer. I think it is arrogant to mutilate people's names for the sake of convenience. We would not like it if other people treated our poets and politicians in the same manner, calling Milton *Milt*, Coleridge *Cole* and Mrs Thatcher *Thatch*.)

The Greeks and the Romans were not ashamed of enjoying something enjoyable, and therefore they enjoyed sex. Heterosexual and homosexual love were equally acceptable. If you were drunk you pleased Bacchus, if you chased beautiful women you pleased Venus. Whatever dirty tricks you got up to, you always pleased at least one of the many Gods. The Gods, by the way, behaved just as badly as humans, and Goddesses were no better than Gods – although for some mysterious reason women are generally supposed to be more restrained and more virtuous than men, a belief not supported either by reason or by evidence.

The Ten Commandments produced by Moses and allegedly given to him by God himself (there were no independent witnesses to that) forbid fornication, which is a mistake. If either Moses or the Almighty had asked for my advice I would have suggested that while promiscuity can be objectionable if pursued in a greedy and selfish way, physical sex when coupled with understanding, gentleness and affection is one of the great gifts to humanity, which should not be referred to by the ugly word fornication. And I would have questioned the good sense of giving something with one hand and taking it back with the other.

The Jews started the Judaeo–Christian–Islamic attitude towards sex, but they were not obsessed by it. I heard once this joke from an old rabbi in Jerusalem.

Cohen went to the synagogue without wearing a hat. The rabbi was outraged and called Cohen in after the service. He was almost speechless with fury. 'To wear no hat in the synagogue . . . That's scandalous . . . That's criminal . . . It's like sleeping with another man's wife.' To which Cohen replied: 'Rabbi, I have tried both. There isn't really any comparison.'

That shows a benevolent, winking tolerance to human frailty. It is Christianity and Islam which have added the element of obsession. The most outstanding theologians give you the impression of having been sex-maniacs. All

they seemed to think about was preventing people from enjoying themselves and procreating their race. It was just such jealous sex-maniacs who had the perverted notion of forbidding priests to marry and produce more priests, worthy men, brought up in a religious atmosphere. Little wonder that this produced (for long centuries) clerics who were lecherous, bishops who lived openly with their concubines, Popes with a string of bastards – and even today ayatollahs who approve and encourage the stoning to death of adulterous women. But not of adulterous men or adulterous ayatollahs.

This confused and hostile attitude to sex created difficulties for Christians when they had to invent God's sex-life.

God is Above Sex (as if to be above sex were a Good Thing). Yet, He has a son. How to explain this? It is not easy, but I could have thought of many better explanations than the Church Fathers succeeded in hitting upon. Now God has a son and this son's mother is a human woman married to another chap. God, however, would not dream of committing adultery, and neither would Mary. There was conception, yes, but it was immaculate. How this is done is not crystal clear – this was the one and only immaculate conception we have ever heard of. One or two women, greatly embarrassed by the birth of a baby while their husbands were away for a few years fighting in the Crusades, tried to put across the same story, but no one believed them. Mary was the only woman who ever got away with it. Not that Mary was not an absolutely virtuous woman. She was. All I suggest is that her husband had more to do with her natural and maculate conception than God.

So, according to Christian theology, God is unmarried but He has a son. Mary had a son but her husband was not the child's father. 'What a family!' you would be inclined to think. But you were taught that this is the most admirable, the most sacred and most wonderful family that ever lived. Joseph was made a saint, which is more than other cuckolded husbands could hope for.

What a dreary God Christians and Muslims have

produced for themselves! Greek and Roman Gods had innumerable affairs and intrigues, and were often unfaithful to their Goddesses who were no better than they. Their affairs would have been too much for the nosiest gossip columnist and too intricate and involved even for Iris Murdoch. But those boring, ascetic, humourless sexmaniacs, the Christian founding fathers and theologians, felt compelled to create an unfortunate God who was permitted one single sex-act in all eternity. And even that one act had to be by proxy.

The Cross God Has to Bear

God has Her problems.

The worst of them is the Church. All Churches: Islamic, Jewish, Shinto, the Church of Rome, Canterbury, Moscow – all of them.

God was first created by nice, simple frightened men who were desperate to find explanations for various terrifying phenomena and were keen on avoiding their inevitable death.

Then the Church stepped in and spoilt God's character and image. The Church did its best to identify itself with God and this was disastrous for God's reputation.

I shall not try to analyse the Bible or to give here even a sketchy history of the Roman Church. I shall simply touch on a few outstanding points or events – to give a taste of the confusion created.

The Bible was the earliest mess learned churchmen created. It is full of contradictions and absurdities. God, according to Genesis, created light on the First Day. If so, who created darkness before? More surprisingly, She created the Sun (and other stars) on the Fourth Day. What gave the light in the first three days?

One day, a few years ago, there was complete bedlam at my place. The telephone kept ringing, the postman, the milkman, the electric meter-reader and some neighbours all called at the same time. Parcels arrived and I had a lot to do. Then a policeman rang my bell and asked me to move a car which was not even mine. In the middle of all this turmoil the bell rang again. I opened the door and

there were two strangers standing in front of it, a black man and a white woman. Both were well dressed and extremely courteous. The black man asked me:

'May we come in and talk to you about the Bible?'

'Not now,' I replied in horror.

'Why not now?'

'Because I am terribly busy.'

'I see,' he said somewhat condescendingly, 'you haven't got a few minutes for God?'

He did not look like God to me, but I let that pass. I apologised and repeated that I was too busy just now and could not discuss the Bible with them. But they would not take no for an answer. They insisted that nothing was more important than the Bible and that one's soul must have priority over all earthly frivolities. They indicated, very politely, that my choice was between letting them in to discuss the Bible then and there and eternal damnation. I chose eternal damnation and told them: 'Look, I didn't mean to upset you but, if I must, I'll give you my real reasons. I am a very virtuous man, a true puritan. The Bible, I am afraid, is full of salacious and scandalous stories and I just would not let that book into my house. Good-bye.'

They looked a little puzzled but left.

* * *

Christians maintain – like all the bigoted followers of other religions – that their faith is the only true one, but they cannot agree among themselves even on the most basic proposition: what *is* their faith? Who is a Christian? Some Christians regard certain doctrines as God's most sacred will, others regard the same as heresy and the road to hell. They have often got down to killing each other with zest and pleasure because of some tiny differences in interpretation. The difference of a single *iota* in two Greek words once cost thousands of lives.

82

The Church has always had an inclination to support the most backward, reactionary and cruel causes throughout the ages. They praised the poor and sided with power. Joachim Kahl writes in his *The Misery of Christianity*:

'. . . the religion which peddles the love of one's fellow-man has, from its earliest beginning right up to the present day, tolerated, encouraged and even committed the most inhuman atrocities in the name of God.'

Just a quick look. The New Testament condemns in strong terms illicit sexual intercourse or *the wearing of long hair* by women, but does not have a word against slavery. Indeed, the early Church (and not only the early one) supported slavery whole-heartedly. Paul's advice to slaves was: 'Submit yourselves voluntarily to your masters in the spirit of humble obedience', and other church-fathers repeated this advice for long centuries. The New Testament orders slaves to be obedient even to the worst masters and accept punishment even if they are innocent. Tertullian – writes Kahl – tried to persuade slaves that freedom and servitude on this earth was meaningless. When the movement for the abolition of slavery gained momentum, the Church declared that the liberation of its slaves was impossible because it was not the Church but God who owned them. Poor God – She did not only approve of slavery but was turned into the largest slave-owner in the world. The Benedictines of Brazil owned slaves (of course, on God's behalf) until 1864. Perhaps this whole attitude has something to do with the fact that the higher clergy were noblemen: slave-owners and not slaves.

Other Christians were no better. Luther, too, justified slavery, using sound theological arguments.

* * *

The Church has a terrifying record in the persecution of pagans and the persecution of Jews (although it took over many pagan doctrines and rites and although Christ was a Jew himself). It is a sad record from the earliest days up to the Concordat with Hitler. God's only son was sent down to earth to die a horrible death – something I would never do to my only son, but then I am not renowned for my Infinite Goodness. The Jews obliged by providing the death . . . and just imagine what would have happened if they had failed. God's plan would have miscarried, the whole scheme would have collapsed, and there would be no Christianity today. But instead of thanking the Jews for this murder, the Christians blamed them severely. The Church has not had a great deal to say about the killing of six million Jews, but the killing of that one Jew has been harped on for nearly two thousand years, thus keeping anti-Semitism alive and burning. Finally – innumerable pogroms, massacres and holocausts later – the Church issued a statement saying that the Jews had not, after all, been responsible for Christ's death. They admitted this as reluctantly as they had admitted that the earth, perhaps, was not flat after all. Both admissions said too little and said it too late. Not a record to be proud of; and to that we have to add the treatment of heretics and witches.

'Heretics' and 'witches' were arrested on the flimsiest of grounds and were regarded as guilty from the outset. They were kept in chains and could not rely on defending counsel. No one would dare to speak for them in any case because anyone who had a good word for a heretic or a witch would be regarded as a heretic himself. Pope Innocent IV issued a bull (in 1252) and regulated the use of torture:

> 'The heretic was dragged into the torture chamber [writes Kahl] and shown all the terrible instruments of torture. If this was not enough and failed to impress the instruments were applied to his body, one by one, producing increasing pain. The rack and other instruments of torture were frequently sprinkled with holy water. A heretic might be tortured for hours until his body became a flayed, bruised, broken and bleeding mass of flesh. In the end he always "confessed" and said what the inquisitor wanted him to say.'

The so-called crimes were either pure inventions or ridiculous fabrications. It was a heretical crime to preach poverty and demand that the Church should give up its tremendous wealth. St Francis of Assissi himself escaped by the skin of his teeth. A Dutch lawyer, John of Oldenharneveldt was burnt because he taught that Christ had died to redeem *all* mankind. True, the Inquisitor handed over his victim to the secular arm but that only meant adding hypocrisy to the other crimes. Pope Paul IV, in the sixteenth century, made his infamous declaration: 'Even if my own father were a heretic I would gladly gather wood to have him burnt.' (Perhaps he hated his father. Some people, as Freud explained later, do.)

I do not want to dwell on the horrors of the *auto-da-fé*, only to add this: Stalin's trials were mild and humane affairs compared with the trials of the Inquisition, and claimed fewer victims. Even Hitler's extermination camps, at least in one respect, were less cruel: the Nazis killed their victims first, the Inquisition burnt them alive.

The Church remained faithful to its traditions right up to our times. Pope Pius XII did not have a word to say about Auschwitz but when the Supreme Court of Yugoslavia sentenced Archbishop Stepinac, a repulsive war criminal, not to death but to a mere sixteen years in prison, the Pope created him a Cardinal for his great services to the Church.

The present Pope lives, of course, in changed times. He loves travelling (perhaps the only possible way of travelling for a Pole is to have himself elected Pope and then set forth on his journeys). Whenever he arrives somewhere – anywhere – he kisses the tarmac of the airport with a passion quite unusual in a Pope. His travelling mania and his kissing of tarmacs are his only innovation. Otherwise his views on sex, marriage, abortion and women's rights are worthy of his medieval predecessors.

* * *

Do I mean to say that all the Church does is wicked and outmoded? Do I mean that all priests are reactionary devils who would still trump up charges and burn people on the scaffold if they had a chance?

Not at all. I have known many priests. I went to school for some years to Cistercian monks and I think of them – well, most of them – with gratitude and affection. I know many other decent, charming and humane priests – many parish priests among them – who are passionately and touchingly devoted to their pastoral duties and work harder than most of us. For years I have been (and still am) a governor of a Catholic school. It is an excellent school, probably one of the best in the country. I shall resign my governorship before the publication of this book because I do not want to embarrass the priests and my colleagues on the board. I should like to say, however, that I have always taken my duties seriously, was deeply impressed by the high standards aimed at and, indeed, achieved, and although not a believer myself I fully agree that any parent who desires a Catholic education for his or her child should have it. I did my best as a governor and shall be sorry to leave.

So if priests – many of them – are such excellent, cultured and humane people, how is it possible that the Church itself is such a non-caring, selfish, greedy and often cruel – indeed murderous – organisation?

The explanation is quite simple. Nowadays it is fashionable to draw a distinction between the 'government' and the 'people'. The priests are the people; the Churches (Rome, Canterbury, Teheran etc) are the governments.

This, however, is not a fully satisfactory explanation. People can be stupid and bloody awful, and a government may be much better than they are. It would be quite useful if Brecht's suggestion could be put into practice: if the government could dissolve the people and elect a new people. Or, at least, we may say that most people get the government they deserve.

I think Frigyes Karinthy, a brilliant Hungarian writer of the first half of this century, gave a convincing explanation to this riddle in a short story entitled 'Christ or Barabbas'.

The Roman official (I think Pilate himself) was prepared to show clemency to one of his prisoners: either to Jesus, King of the Jews, or to Barabbas, the thief. He asked the excited crowd who should go free: Christ or Barabbas? All *individuals* shouted: Christ! Yet, the thunderous reply of the *crowd* was: Barabbas! This is the real explanation. All these nice, decent priests shout: Christ! But the roar of the Church is: Barabbas!

87

Superstition?

A somewhat pompous Catholic dignitary told me: 'There is no conflict between science and religion. Superstition is the common enemy of both.'

This is a ludicrous statement. How dare the Church who persecuted Galileo, decried Darwin, fought Freud etc etc suggest such a thing? The fact that the Church has always been beaten and forced to retreat in its battles against science certainly does not mean that there never has been a conflict.

The great meeting point between science and religion is – or is supposed to be – theology. Theology is – they say – the science of religion. Except that it isn't. Theology is not a science, indeed there is nothing scientific about it. It is a great pity that so many first-rate brains (forgetting now about the second- and third-rate ones) have devoted themselves to explaining the inexplicable, proving the unprovable and relying on 'evidence' which would have been thrown out even by the lowest court in the Balkans in the last century.

But I am even more annoyed – or amused – by another aspect of this boast that superstition is the enemy both of science and religion. Superstition is not the enemy of the

Church but its best friend, most important ally and mainstay.

What is superstition? It depends on the Church which defines it. To speak of Heaven and Hell is sheer superstition in the eyes of a Hindu who knows – it has all been scientifically proved by Hindu theologians – that the soul is reincarnated and sometimes we appear on this earth as human beings, sometimes as beetles and sometimes as rattlesnakes. In the eyes of a Christian, to believe in more Gods than one – to accept polytheism – is sheer pagan superstition; but to believe in three Gods rolled into one is not only the declared Truth but is monotheism. (Some Chinese restaurants serve a soup called 'Three in One'. It consists of three constituent elements but it is, really, one soup. This is the doctrine of the Holy Trinity translated into Chinese cooking.)

The Greeks and the Romans were pagans because they believed that various aspects of human activity had each its own God. This was a childish mistake made by primitive peoples. But people who would hotly deny that they are primitive – Catholics today – believe that various groups or functions such as the poor, merchants, travellers, adventurers and so on, have their protective saints. To pray to Hermes or Mercury (who, among other things was a great traveller, being the Messenger of the Gods) is pagan superstition; to pray to St Christopher, protecting saint of travellers, is a reasonable act, approved by scientifically minded theologians.

Any Hindu will tell you that refusing to eat pork is a childish superstition; it is beef you must not touch. (By the way, you must not eat pork because it is unclean and you must not eat beef because the cow is sacred. Some monkeys are also sacred but you may eat them.)

Moses was worried that eating pork under the blazing sun of the desert was very unhealthy for his wandering tribes, so he made God forbid the consumption of pork. A wise move in the circumstances. Now, a few thousand years on, in the Age of Frozen Food, the Jews of New York and London still refuse to eat pork because it was unhealthy in the Sinai Desert during forty years of wandering a few millennia ago. But this is not superstition: it is obeying the will of the Almighty.

Just as it is the will of Jehova and Allah that Jews and Muslims should slaughter animals in a special way. Ritual slaughter is a bit of a puzzle. It may be crueller than ordinary slaughter – as its opponents declare – or it may be less cruel as its practitioners maintain. But when battery chicken-farmers, bull-fighters, fur-traders, animal experimenters and vivisectionists are worried about the suffering caused by ritual slaughter, their motives seem a little suspect. Perhaps it is sheer superstition.

Mohammed ordered that the women of Islam must cover their faces. The ayatollahs of Iran and other Muslim fundamentalists believe that this law is of overwhelming importance. I have seen many beautiful Arab and other Eastern ladies, but some ungallant Westerners remarked that Mohammed's wisest law has been to cover up the faces of Oriental ladies.

When a devout Christian is shown the cave of Pythia in Delphi, he smiles superciliously at the naivety of those heathens; but when some devout monk in Jerusalem shows him (for a consideration) the footprints of the Archangel Gabriel in the rock, he crosses himself.

So one man's superstition is another man's sacred belief, even his scientific doctrine. Which would do no harm if the priests, rabbis, imams, Buddhist and other monks etc did not take it so deadly seriously. If one person refuses to eat *Wiener Schnitzel*, that is his business; if another prays to St Christopher before a journey – let him. I fully agree with the little boy of whom Sir Arthur Evans, the great archaeologist, related this story.

Evans visited a small village somewhere in Crete and attended the service of the Orthodox Church. A little boy was carrying the incense-burner and murmuring something as he swung it – the same brief sentence over and over again. Evans knew Greek well but could not catch a single word of what the boy was saying. After the service, he asked the priest what sort of Cretan dialect the little boy was speaking.

'It is not a Cretan dialect,' replied the priest. 'He speaks English. He is a Scottish boy whom we picked up after a shipwreck and kept in the monastery.'

Evans was surprised. 'Scottish? What were the words he was repeating?'

The priest explained that he himself did not know English, but the words murmured by the boy sounded something like: 'It does no good, it does no harm . . . It does no good, it does no harm . . .'

Pension Her Off!

————◆————

So if it does no good and does no harm then what am I complaining about? Why do I bother to think about the Church? And at this stage, as I am speaking personally, I mean the Church as I know it best – the Church in Europe, not as it exists in other parts of the world.

First of all I think the Church, unlike incense, does both harm and good. About the harm I have already made a brief and sketchy resumé. I could write a whole book about it – much longer than this one – and, indeed, many people have done so. The good the Church does is mostly incidental – with one single exception. Individual priests and monks, as I have said earlier, are full of goodwill and often perform good and noble deeds. While, during the last war, the Pope was flirting with the Nazis, many priests, monks and nuns were hiding persecuted Jews at great personal risk to themselves. (And so, for that matter, were many convinced and steadfast atheists.)

In earlier times the Church was the only source of learning and knowledge. It abused its position, tried to prevent knowledge from spreading and thus lost its monopoly, but for a long time, being a learned man meant to be a priest, and all universities were run by the Church. Quite often, of course, they spread false knowledge and downright ignorance, but European scholarship and culture have their roots in those distant times when the Church was the sole depository of knowledge and learning.

The Church pretends to be the guardian of goodness, tolerance, understanding – all the virtues. A priest is supposed to be a decent, caring and lovable man, watching us fallible mortals with tolerant eyes and a paternal, understanding smile. Well, many priests, as I said above, are like that, but many others are quarrelsome, vain, competitive, over-ambitious, greedy, jealous and self-indulgent phoneys. And even if the Church really did embody goodness – which it doesn't – it would have no monopoly of goodness.

The one truly great service that religion does to humanity is that it exists. Because religion is badly needed. Not this or that religion in particular, but some sort of religion. I shall have more to say about substitute religions in the next chapter but at the moment let us stick to 'religion' in the accepted sense of the word.

Once I was at a party attended by several priests and nuns. Someone quoted a person who had made some sort of anti-religious remark or joke – I do not remember the actual words. One of the nuns exclaimed, 'How stupid! When I think of all the comfort I have had from religion throughout my life!'

That was a simple, honest, heartfelt cry from a simple and honest woman. But how revealing it is. How sincere and how selfish at one and the same time. She stuck to religion, remained a believer – indeed, became a nun – not because it was true, not because all her doubts had been dispelled after thorough reflection, but because religion gave her comfort and sweetened her life. Since life can often do with sweetening, it must be granted that the Church is doing something useful in providing it – but although I am happy to admit that, I would be happier if the Church admitted it too. Valium may be a wonderful tranquilliser but it does not pretend to be the Universal Truth.

The trouble with the whole concept – Church and God – is that it has become old-fashioned, out-of-date. The Church is no longer the depository of knowledge and culture; it is not – it has never been, really, the incarnation of goodness; it is not the main source of friendly advice –

Citizens' Advice Bureaux, solicitors, and various other kinds of consultant beat it hands down. The Church is fading rapidly in importance.

Few people in Western Europe really care about religion one way or another. They are busy with more important things (business, watching the telly, going to the pub, discussing politics, playing bridge). A dwindling number of true believers go to Church and some others go too, to be seen there, to conform, or out of habit or to listen to local gossip. A few even go to pray. Hats off to that tiny minority. Otherwise the Church is invaded from time to time by non-believers who go there to get married, to have their children christened and to get buried. Why not? It does no good, it does no harm as that small Scottish boy so rightly remarked. The marriage ceremony is more impressive at a Church than at a registry office; it may be to your child's advantage to get baptised; and one must be buried or burnt somewhere – it is very unhygienic not to be.

Even so – and this is rather extraordinary – it still takes a bit of courage to stand up against religion, even today. To remain neutral, to say 'Oh, I'm no regular churchgoer but, I suppose, I believe in God', is acceptable in most communities. Others demand a more positive approach. You must turn up in church every Sunday and proclaim your faith unequivocally. Should you refuse, you court ostracism, paternal opprobrium, possibly the break-up of the family and economic disaster. So a small percentage of people pretend to believe although they do not. A much larger percentage of these religious communities – perhaps a majority – are more honest and refuse to pretend. So to avoid the dangers and yet to remain honest, they choose a simple way out: they persuade themselves that they are true and honest believers. It is, after all, much simpler to *believe that you believe* than to face the wrath of the bigots, outrage your community, upset your family and lose your job. Why should one do that? For the sake of something so unimportant as religion has become for most people? Just to avoid a few boring hours in church? The sermon may be dull but the post-service gossip is, as a rule, full compensation for it.

How can I tell – the reader may ask – the true believer from the person who has succeeded in persuading himself that he *is* a true believer? Of course I cannot. Neither can he. Nor is it necessary. A man who sincerely believes that he is a true believer *is* a true believer. At the bottom of his heart he may be a coward. But he is a *true* coward.

I must repeat: I do not deny the existence of honest and sincere believers. But people in whose life religion is the guiding light are members of a dwindling band.

So humanity is slowly, very slowly, growing up. It is growing out of fairy tales. It does not need the Church any more and it does not bother to say so loudly and clearly because it's not worth the trouble. The controversy tends to become acrimonious and the Church refuses to do the decent thing: to shut up shop. The Church is rich; it employs hundreds of thousands of people; and its main justification is that it has gone on for a long time so that, it feels, it should go on forever. The Church, like most of us, is inclined to believe that two thousand years is a long time. It isn't, of course; it's nothing . . . but people are inclined to believe that something that has existed all their lifetime, is eternal. I was born in the Austro-Hungarian Empire. It looked as strong, as powerful and as everlasting as the Church. Before I reached the ripe old age of seven, it had disappeared and today it is a fading memory, mostly in the minds of historians, like the Roman Empire is and the British Empire will soon be. The Church *will* disappear in time, but not yet. The passion of the Pope for kissing tarmac is a powerful passion.

People do not fight against their respective Churches because they do not feel that the Churches really matter. And they are good for ceremony, pageantry, royal weddings and the tourist trade. And if people feel this 'couldn't care less' way about their Churches, they inevitably feel rather the same about God.

God is getting old. She has, of course, always been old. This is not a gallant thing to say about a lady, but if She has been living since eternity, then She has no beginnings and She must *always* have been old. It is a concept somewhat difficult for our finite minds to grasp, but if the existence of God has no end it has no beginning either. (The beginning of eternity is as difficult a notion as the idea of infinite smallness. We can imagine something infinitely long or huge, but not infinitely small, because the infinitely small seems to be nothing. But it isn't. The millionth of a second does not last long but it is a measurable lapse of time. And even that is not infinitely small, because half of a millionth of a second is a shorter period still.)

God, then, was *born* old. We all know people who were born old and remained old people all their lives, but ordinary people have a chronological age in addition to a real one. God has always been *chronologically* old. This did not matter at first. In spite of Her respectable age, She could remain young and powerful for a long time. But now She has become old-fashioned; not only old but elderly; not only ancient but belonging to a bygone era.

Humanity created God and it could kill Her off. But murder is a nasty business and God deserves a better fate. She has served us well. No, She must not be treated unkindly. She should be retired. Voluntary redundancy would be preferable but if She insists on going on She must be pensioned off. Her activities, Her interference with our lives must cease, because humanity *must* slowly grow up. Perhaps it never will, but it ought to. Let's let God go on with Her everlasting life in peaceful retirement. Let Her enjoy Herself. Some people will still care for Her, will still pray to Her, with luck enough of them to keep Her happy. We *want* Her to be happy, content. She was the best God we had. But the all-powerful, revengeful, whimsical, thunderous and humourless Almighty should be transformed into the Eternal Old Age Pensioner. Amen.

Gods that Failed

Nearly all religious teaching and belief is based on cowardice. Humanity is afraid of death; and is afraid of life.

Religion is the Great Tranquilliser, the Universal Valium and it has two tremendous advantages: it reassures people that they will live forever or will be resurrected after their death, although it is made clear that they must pay for their sins on this earth.

But let us examine the fear of life first. The great strength of religion is that it claims the whole man, that it rules people's entire life and – even more important – it can answer all the questions life may pose to them. In many cases religion gives a patently wrong, old-fashioned, out-dated answer to our questions: in sexual matters, for example, nearly all religions are a few centuries behind the times, our own Western ones especially so. But even if dogmatic answers to sexual problems are given by people who – in the same breath – tell us that they never had any sexual experience and have never been married, there are still many people who feel that a silly answer is preferable to no answer at all. If there is one thing that humanity abhors more than death it is responsibility. So an institution that professes to know all the answers to all our problems is most welcome. On top of it all, you may feel virtuous because you are told that you are obeying God's own will.

The difficulty for religion is that many other doctrines have sprung up which also demand total devotion and which also have answers for all the problems of life. Marxism is one, a modern religion, a powerful rival of the old one. Arthur Koestler described the process of his conversion to Marxism:

'Every page of Marx and even more of Engels, brought a new discovery and an intellectual delight . . . By the time I had finished with Engel's *Feuerbach* and Lenin's *State and Revolution* something had clicked in my brain and I was shaken by a mental explosion. To say that one had "seen the light" is a poor description of the intellectual rapture which only the convert knows (regardless to what faith he has been converted). The new light seems to pour in from all directions, the whole universe falls into pattern like the stray pieces of the jigsaw puzzle, assembled by magic at one stroke. There is now an answer to every question . . .'

What is this if not religious conversion?

Little wonder that Marxism and religion have turned against each other. They had to. Both demanded the full man; neither could be content with a half.

Another religion-substitute – older than Marxism but younger than Christianity – is nationalism: a God that was most powerful in the nineteenth century and in the first half of the present century, but which has lost almost as much prestige recently as the God in Heaven. Nationalism – unlike Marxism – concluded a close alliance with the Churches which, in turn, always supported nationalism, in all countries, however hostile to one another. During the First World War the Churches in Germany prayed for a German victory, while those in France and Britain prayed for an Allied victory, each side assuring its combatants that Truth and God were with them. Hitler, who took nationalism to its mad but logical conclusion, realised that a total devotion to Nazism was incompatible with a total devotion to God, so he became

jealous of God, whom he was determined to replace. And he nearly did.

Freudian (and post-Freudian, Jungian, Kleinian etc) psychology is another aspirant to religious status. Charles Rycroft (in *The God I Want*) writes:

'It must be remembered that he [Freud] . . . founded a movement with its own hierarchy and its own form of Apostolic Succession and the Laying on of Hands – the training in analysis means that all Freudian analysts can trace their descent from either Freud himself or one of the original "disciples" and that he devised a new set of myths and symbols which bid fair to replace the traditional Christian iconography.'

Psychology, indeed, tries to replace religion even harder than most other movements. It cannot share supremacy with traditional religion and it dubs religion a 'wish-fulfilling illusion' (which, of course, it is). But it goes a few steps further. Analysts are often regarded by their patients – and often regard themselves – as substitute Gods. Rycroft again:

'. . . he [the analyst] comes to believe that he is the sole fount of insight, wisdom and light.'

Humanity goes on and on with its search for substitute religions. It needs a guide for *all* its problems. That is why so many crazy sects flourish. Right down in the rank of substitutes lurk the football hooligans: they are not just bloodthirsty revolutionaries or mindless vandals, they are lost souls searching for an answer. Why are the English the leading hooligans? The English have given many wonderful and popular sports to the world, football hooliganism is just another addition to the list even if it can hardly be called a desirable exercise. It has its rules – like all games – although these rules are somewhat novel and not traditional: always kick the man who is down; hold a man's arm while your pal cuts his face; bite off your opponent's ears etc.

All the Single Issue Fanatics (Bernard Levin's phrase) are in a desperate search for a cause which may fill their empty lives and give them some meaning, guidance and purpose.

Religion and all its substitutes represent not only a desperate thirst for guidance; they claim more than the entire being of their followers. They become, much too often, dangerous, destructive forces, a real menace to all of us.

Nice, decent, cultured and soft-hearted people, as soon as they feel that they represent some abstract idea – be it the Cross, the Bible, the Koran, a Class, a Nation, Liberty, Fraternity, Equality or Animal Rights – become murderous beasts. They are ready to kill and ready to die for their monomania which seems to them the final, absolute, irrefutable truth. The messianic man – whatever his mission – whether he is an Imam or a Crusader against the ritual slaughter of chickens – does no less harm than many of the other groups which he contemptuously dismisses as terrorists.

* * *

If . . . . There used to be a saying in Vienna: 'If my grandmother had had four wheels she would have been an omnibus.' Quite. If humanity had the sense and courage commensurate with its technical brilliance it would be quite a commendable humanity and it would by now have thrown away religion as a growing child throws away his rattle. Priests would admit that religions are based on sheer invention, unworthy of intelligent, grown-up people, would dissolve their orders and would turn their churches into museums, hospitals, supermarkets or theatres and would go out to find – or try to find – worthwhile jobs. Perhaps a minority of truly good Church men would continue with its good work without the hocus-pocus of religious ceremonies, and without such rituals as eating Christ's body and drinking his blood.

In the fifties Ceslav Milos, the excellent Polish writer who about thirty years later won the Nobel Prize for Literature, escaped from his native land and published a brilliant and frightening analysis of Stalinism. He stated that there were a hundred and one basic tenets of the Creed and if someone doubted a single one of them he was branded a traitor to Communism and thrown into prison or, perhaps, tortured to death. No one, not even Stalin himself, believed in all the hundred and one dogmas but *all behaved as if they did*. People who did not believe in the Creed persecuted and prosecuted others who did not believe in it either. This was an era, said Milos, when strict orthodoxy was maintained by a gang of unbelievers.

Similarly, there is not one person – I feel sure – in the whole of our clergy who believes all the Church's dogmas unhesitatingly without a shadow of doubt. The Bishop of Durham is only one example – though an important one. Modern Christianity has become the Faith of the Unbelievers. And so, no doubt, have most other religions.

If some people *need* religion, let them have it by all means. People are allowed – and they should be allowed – to found spiritualist circles, so they should also be allowed to form other groups which believe in the resurrection of Christ and in everlasting life. But they should do it at their own expense, not at mine. I do not doubt that deep religious convictions are held by many excellent people. I fully respect their convictions. All I am asking in exchange is that they should respect my atheist conviction and acknowledge that it can be held with an honesty and integrity equal to their own. It may turn out to be my misfortune, but it is certainly not my crime, not to have believed in a man who was really a God, born of a virgin mother.

* * *

General resurrection could be quite an embarrassing business. There are enough Chinese in the world as it is. Imagine *all* the Chinese ever born, crowded together in China. And why pick on China? If all the people who ever lived were brought back to life again they would pose quite a problem to the welfare state.

Resurrection would be embarrassing in many other ways, too. Think of those reunions with our loved ones. Not every family was a happy, united family but let us take the happy and united ones. I loved my father dearly and think of him with a great deal of gratitude and affection. He died when I was a boy of ten, i.e. more than sixty years ago. I just would not know what to say to him if we met again. If he asked me about my life and I told him that, as a matter of fact, I became an English writer in London, he would burst into tears. What a terrible disappointment: his eldest son, whom he meant to bring up as a decent and honest citizen, must have become a bloody liar, and is trying to fool his own father after our common resurrection. What could I say to Harry, my two-year-old grandson, who will hardly remember the old boy who came to visit him and his elder brother about once a fortnight in the nineteen-eighties and tried to entertain him with silly jokes – found irresistibly funny at the time? What could Harry say to me? Would it be a happy reunion of loved ones or a pretty embarrassing bore where everybody felt that it was his bounden duty to enjoy himself but couldn't?

To meet Ginger, my recently departed cat, would be an entirely different proposition. We could continue our relationship where we left off. He would jump on my lap and I would stroke his beautiful blond head. But Ginger will not be resurrected because he has no soul. I have no soul either; I don't need one and I would not know what to do with it.

The great difference between me and religious people is this: they cannot be disappointed and proved wrong but I can. If they die and that is the end of it all, they will not be able to complain to anyone, they will never even become aware of the fact that they gave their life and their honest conviction to a false creed. But if God does exist and confronts me, after my death, with a wagging finger and an ironic smile on Her lips, asking: 'Well, do I exist after all?' – I will really not know what to reply.

On Real Immortality

Some people may think: what a dreary, gloomy, mournful outlook mine is compared with the happy, bright and exhilarating promises of the Church. But, in fact, it is the other way round. The boot is on the other foot.

Is it really so wonderful or virtuous to mislead yourself and others with childish and implausible promises and hopes? Is it not more courageous to face reality, particularly when reality seems to me more pleasant than the promised bliss? *This is your life.* You make it or mar it here, on this earth. At one of the ancient Olympic Games an athlete – a long-jumper from Rhodes – performed miserably. As an excuse he stuttered something about having jumped much better at home in Rhodes. To which someone replied: 'Hic Rhodos, hic salta!' That's what we have to tell ourselves and all our fellow-humans on this earth: 'Rhodes is here, it's here we have to jump.'

How many millions have been cheated, fooled, bullied into a miserable existence, condemned to poverty, slavery and injustice because they were forced to believe that Rhodes was not here but in Never-Never Land. People gave up the joys of life, the pleasure and beauty of sex and family life, soldiers eagerly rushed to their deaths for rewards that never came.

Man (and I mean, of course, women too) should face the idea of death not only bravely but with joy. There is nothing wrong with total and final extinction after a long and happy life. A life cut short by illness or accident is a tragedy – but rarely an unmitigated tragedy without consolation. But even a total tragedy cannot be put right by the fairy tale that all other creatures on this planet (and millions of other planets) are mortal but one single animal on this one single insignificant planet will enjoy eternal life. In this case the old saying is literally true: if you can believe that you can believe anything. Death is the full stop at the end of the sentence (in both meanings of the word) and makes our life full and complete.

Whatever has a beginning must have an end. And so it should be. Who wants to live forever, in Paradise or on this earth, listening to bad music played by amateur harp-players and living in conditions more overcrowded than those in that other earthly Paradise, Moscow? Millions and millions of people (dead – even if resurrected) and living squeezed together? People who have nothing to say to one another? No – one of the beauties of life is death.

To those who cannot give up the idea of immortality, who must cling to it, I say this: *do not worry, we are all immortal*. We are immortal in a more pleasant and lovely way than that described in the Bible, the Koran or any other so-called sacred book.

Some people try to preserve their body after death but what happens to one's body should be a matter of total indifference. My body, without my heart beating and my brain working, is not me. The morbid preoccupation with cemeteries, tombs, graves, *pompes funèbres* is just another expression of fear. We do not even mourn the dead; we mourn ourselves. Every funeral is our own funeral; every grave is our own grave.

I do not speak of the immortality of the body. I am not worried even about the bodies of missionaries eaten by cannibals. Omnipotent God – if She exists – will paste them together somehow. Even She will not find it easy, but She can do it. I don't want flowers on my grave; only symbolic mental flowers on my memory.

When I die (and this goes for all of us) I shall be remembered by a few friends, perhaps rather more women than men, who liked me a little and will spare a kind thought for the departed. 'He was a bastard but he could be quite amusing', one of them may say. 'He was kind to his cats', another may say. 'The *Wiener Schnitzel* he made was out of this world', may be contributed by a third. And as long as the memory of my life and *my Wiener Schnitzel* survives I am not dead. To live in the hearts of your friends who really cared for you – with warts and all – is the only kind of immortality worth aspiring to.

You carry in yourself the immortality of your forebears and you too will survive in your children, grandchildren and great-grandchildren. You keep erecting monuments to yourself; not only in so-called works of art, but a garden here, an originally furnished room there, a few remarks you made, a few good deeds you did. If you have helped someone to a little happiness he will think of you with gratitude after your death – however hard he tried to avoid such feelings while you were alive. If you have written, painted, built something or created something in any way you will live on in your creation for ten, a hundred or a thousand years. It does not really matter how long, the difference between ten and a thousand is much smaller than it looks from where we are sitting.

'But even a thousand years is not forever,' you may object, you greedy thing. No, it isn't. But, believe me, even eternity does not last forever.

* * *

'Man is mortal but the world will go on forever' – this is the general belief. But it is really the other way round.

There is no such thing as *the* world. The world is a subjective perception. We all look at it from behind our own eyes; *the* world is *our* world, different from the many millions of worlds belonging to other people. When our consciousness ceases, whatever happens to us, our world dies – and dies forever. It will never be resurrected. Many thousands of worlds die every day, but our smiles, our modest good deeds, our small kindnesses, our few and limited achievements make *us* immortal. Not *very* immortal; but a bit immortal.

* * *

Even God – whether this little book causes Her immediate demise or is thrown away with a yawn – yes, even God is not immortal. At the best She will live as long as humanity does: another few million years. Quite a while in human terms but a brief moment in the life of a God.

So better to pension Her off decently and straight away. She was a good God, as Gods go. Her various Churches often dragged Her name in the mud but She did Her best in difficult circumstances – Her shortcomings were our fault, not Hers. She served us well; She deserved better. *Requiescat in pace.* She should rest in peace. She deserves it.

. . . But before we let Her go, I would like to address just one short letter to Her – a personal one.

Dear God,

I shall address this letter to 'Everywhere' because I do not know your private address. I know it's supposed to be Heaven, but that's so vague: where is Heaven? Earlier generations thought it was above the clouds, but in this age of aeroplanes we have all been above the clouds. Sometimes we found Hell there, but never Heaven. Besides, it takes the Post Office a very long time to convey a letter from Fulham to Putney, so how long would it take for a letter to get from Fulham to Heaven? Considering that You, if You exist, are omnipresent, 'Everywhere' seemed to me the best address. Sorry I don't know the post code.

At the beginning of this book I said that in Part Two I would give You some advice on how to be God. I have, in fact, more or less done so, but I should like to be a little more explicit, and that is why I am venturing to address this letter directly to You.

If You do not exist I can hardly ask You to make Your non-existence clear by some signal. But, after all, those who believe in You may be right and I may be wrong. If You do exist my disbelief would not be the first mistake in my life, nor would it be – I hope – the last one. And it would not, I respectfully submit, really be *my* mistake. Since it is open to You to make me a devout believer, the responsibility would be Yours.

I wish to be brief, so I shall make only three specific points.

1.   Please put Your divine foot down and order a little

more restraint and common sense among Your believers. Tell them to stop fighting one another with all the ferocity and wickedness at their command and blaming it on You. Make it clear that they must bear the responsibility for their own misdeeds and cannot commit endless evil, including mass-murder, in Your name (as given in their various Holy Scriptures). Point out to them that slaughtering people in the name of universal Love is not logical.

2.   Be more scrutable and fathomable. I mean, be less inscrutable and unfathomable. Tell Your followers to stop proclaiming that plague, famine, flood, fire, earthquakes, erupting volcanoes, and millions of children dying of diseases are all the results of Your infinite goodness, and if people fail to understand this it's because Your ways are unfathomable. To my limited human brain sufficient food, health, shelter – even a little comfort, a decent job and the love of our fellow creatures – are all good things, while burning or starving or drowning to death are not so good. So make Your ways a little more fathomable. Please.

3.   Give us a clear sign of Your existence. What about a few miracles? How is it that so many of them occurred in primitive times and none occurs today? I suggest that You perform just a few miracles before a committee composed of selected members of the Royal Society, the faculty of Yale, and that of the Sorbonne. It would be easy for You, and it would settle age-long debates for good. Or perhaps You could send us a second Son of Yours – cause another lady to conceive immaculately. I know it is more difficult to find a virgin today than it used to be, but You are omnipotent, so You could do it. (An age-difference of two thousand years between brothers is, I agree, unusual; but Your family, with all respect, is an unusual family.) True, this would change the Holy Trinity into a Holy Quaternity, but would that matter? It would be child's play for Your theologians to explain that the four of You are really only One. It could be this younger Son of Yours who did

the new and scientifically supervised miracles. He could bring messages from You, and do whatever You and He deemed fit. . . .

. . . But one thing I beg of You: do not let Him save us. If this is what His brother did . . . then this Son must leave us unsaved. And happy. Or at least a little more human.

Until I see these modest requests fulfilled,
I remain
Yours faithlessly

George Mikes